D0033268

MOVIE ★ ICONS

CHAPLIN

EDITOR
PAUL DUNCAN

TEXT
DAVID ROBINSON

PHOTOS
ROY EXPORT COMPANY ESTABLISHMENT

TASCHEN

HONG KONG KÖLN LONDON LOS ANGELES MADRID PARIS TOKYO

CONTENTS

1

CHARLIE CHAPLIN: THE LITTLE FELLOW

BY DAVID ROBINSON

CHARLIE CHAPLIN: DER KLEINE MANN

CHARLIE CHAPLIN : LE PETIT BONHOMME

CHARLIE CHAPLIN: THE LITTLE FELLOW

by David Robinson

More than seventy years since he last appeared on the screen, Charles Chaplin's Little Tramp remains a supreme icon not just of the movies but of the twentieth century – still recognized and loved throughout the world. If there can be an explanation of his unique success with a universal public, it is his gift of transmuting the fundamental anxieties and concerns of human life into comedy – a reflection of his own life experiences. Born in London, the son of music hall singers who separated when he was a baby, he grew up in extreme poverty, spending part of his childhood in institutions for destitute children. At ten years old however his fortunes took an abrupt and significant turn when he became a professional performer. Jobs in music hall troupes and a three-year stint on the legitimate stage gave him a precocious grounding in stagecraft. His gifts were honed by his years with Fred Karno, the most brilliant comedy impresario of the British music halls.

Whilst touring the United States vaudeville circuits he was spotted and engaged by Mack Sennett's Keystone studios. He quickly recognized that to fulfill his own comedy style in films he must be his own director. He mastered the craft of film with phenomenal speed, and after the first three months in pictures was to direct all his own films. Always in search of greater independence, as well as larger salaries, he passed from Keystone in turn to the Essanay and the Mutual film companies. The first four years in pictures saw him develop from the carefree knockabout of the Keystone comedies, to introduce irony and sentiment, and to progress to the Mutual masterpieces that included *The Pawnshop* (1916), *Easy Street* (1917) and *The Immigrant* (1917).

In 1918 an agreement with the distribution company First National enabled him to achieve the luxury of his own studio, designed to be state-of-the-art for its day, and with his

CHAPLIN STUDIOS (c. 1918)
Chaplin controlled every aspect of his films, especially in the cutting room. / Chaplin kontrollierte bei seinen Filmen jeden Aspekt, insbesondere am Schneidetisch. / Chaplin contrôle chaque aspect de ses films, notamment dans la salle de montage.

"[T]hat obstinate, suspicious, egocentric, maddening and lovable genius of a problem child, Charlie Chaplin."
Mary Pickford, 1953

own permanent cast and crew. Here he transmuted the horrors of the First World War into comedy in *Shoulder Arms* (1918) and embodied the privations and anxieties of his own childhood in *The Kid* (1921), in which he found an ideal partner in the 5-year-old Jackie Coogan.

In 1919 the four Hollywood giants of the day – Chaplin, Douglas Fairbanks, Mary Pickford and the director D.W. Griffith – formed United Artists, to distribute their own films. Chaplin's first release through the company was *A Woman of Paris* (1921), a dramatic film designed to star Edna Purviance – his faithful leading lady and sometime love interest since 1915 – in which he made only a fleeting appearance. This brilliant film was a revolution in sophisticated comedy style, but Chaplin's only box-office disaster. It was offset by the triumph of *The Gold Rush* (1925), which again demonstrated Chaplin's belief that tragedy and comedy are never far apart: this hilarious comedy was inspired by the acute privations of gold prospectors of the 1890s.

The arrival of talking pictures in 1927 was a bigger challenge to Chaplin than to most other directors. His wordless pantomime had won a universal audience, which would inevitably shrink if he now spoke in English. Chaplin's response was to continue making silent films – *City Lights* (1931) and *Modern Times* (1936) – with the sound track used only for sound effects and musical accompaniment, the latter composed by Chaplin, adding a new credit to those of producer, director, writer and star.

In *Modern Times* Chaplin brought the comic weapon to bear on burning issues of the day – like industrialization and the confrontation of capital and labor. In *The Great Dictator* (1940) his targets were fascism and its leaders, the gravest peril of the day. Critics complained that the comic was exceeding his function.

Chaplin's unceasing championing of the underdog and his friendships with left-wing intellectuals had always been mistrusted by America's political right wing. With the Cold War and McCarthyist persecution of the political left, Chaplin became a prominent target. *Monsieur Verdoux* (1947), a satirical film which paralleled the activities of a serial killer with the licensed murder of war, drew more ire; and after *Limelight* (1952), a bittersweet recollection of the music halls of his youth, he left America for permanent exile in Switzerland. In London he made two more films: *A King in New York* (1957), a satire on America's political paranoia and *A Countess from Hong Kong* (1967). Indefatigable to the end, he published two autobiographical volumes, composed music for his old silent films, and to the end still planned another film. He died on Christmas Day 1977.

CHARLIE CHAPLIN: DER KLEINE MANN

von David Robinson

Über 70 Jahre, nachdem der kleine Tramp zum letzten Mal über die Leinwand tänzelte, ist er noch immer eine Filmikone und darüber hinaus eine Ikone des 20. Jahrhunderts – die von Charles Chaplin verkörperte Figur ist auf der ganzen Welt bekannt und beliebt. Wenn es eine Erklärung für Chaplins einzigartigen Erfolg bei einem weltweiten Publikum gibt, dann liegt sie in seiner Gabe, die grundlegenden Sorgen und Ängste des menschlichen Lebens in Komik umzuwandeln – als Spiegel seiner eigenen Lebenserfahrungen. Geboren wurde er in London. Seine Eltern waren Varietékünstler und trennten sich, als er noch ein Kleinkind war. Chaplin wuchs in größter Armut auf und verbrachte seine Kindheit teilweise in Heimen für bedürftige Kinder. Als er jedoch im Alter von zehn Jahren erstmals professionell auf der Bühne stand, wendete sich sein Schicksal ganz plötzlich zum Besseren. Jobs bei Varietébühnen und drei Jahre am „richtigen" Theater lehrten ihn frühzeitig die Kunst der Dramaturgie. Die Jahre in den Komikertruppen von Fred Karno, dem genialsten Impresario der britischen Varietészene, gaben seinem Talent den letzten Schliff.

Auf einer Varietétournee durch die Vereinigten Staaten wurde er von Mack Sennetts Keystone-Studios entdeckt und engagiert. Chaplin erkannte sehr schnell, dass er selbst die Regie übernehmen musste, wenn er seinen eigenen Komikstil auf die Leinwand bringen wollte. In erstaunlich kurzer Zeit eignete er sich das Filmhandwerk an, und nach drei Monaten beim Film sollte er bei allen seinen zukünftigen Filmen auch Regie führen. Auf der unablässigen Suche nach größerer Unabhängigkeit und höheren Gagen wechselte er von Keystone zu Essanay und danach zu Mutual. Innerhalb von vier Jahren entwickelten sich seine Filme vom sorglosen Klamauk der Keystone-Klamotten über Komödien mit ironischen und sentimentalen Elementen zu den Meisterwerken der Mutual-Jahre wie *Das Pfandhaus* (1916), *Leichte Straße* (1917) und *Der Einwanderer* (1917).

Im Jahre 1918 konnte er sich dank einer Vertriebsvereinbarung mit dem Verleih First National den Luxus eines eigenen Studios leisten. Es verfügte über den damals neuesten Stand der Technik und arbeitete mit festgestellten Darstellern und Technikern. Hier verarbeitete er die Schrecken des Ersten Weltkriegs in der Komödie *Gewehr über!* (1918) und die Ängste und Entbehrungen seiner eige-

---

„[D]ieses störrische, misstrauische, selbstsüchtige, unerträgliche und liebenswerte Genie von einem Problemkind, Charlie Chaplin."
Mary Pickford, 1953

STILL FROM 'THE CIRCUS' (1928)
So hungry he will steal from a baby. / So hungrig, dass er ein Kind bestiehlt. / Tellement affamé qu'il vole la nourriture d'un enfant.

HAROLD LLOYD, CHARLIE CHAPLIN & DOUGLAS FAIRBANKS (c. 1930)

nen Kindheit in *Der Vagabund und das Kind* (1921), wo er in dem fünfjährigen Jackie Coogan den idealen Leinwandpartner fand.

Im Jahre 1919 gründeten vier Hollywood-Giganten der damaligen Zeit – Chaplin, Douglas Fairbanks, Mary Pickford und der Regisseur D. W. Griffith – die Firma United Artists („vereinigte Künstler"), um die eigenen Filme selbst zu vertreiben. Chaplins erster Film im Verleih der neuen Firma war *Die Nächte einer schönen Frau* (1923). In dem Drama, das Edna Purviance – seiner langjährigen Hauptdarstellerin und seit 1915 für kurze Zeit seine Geliebte – auf den Leib geschrieben war, hatte er nur einen kurzen Auftritt. Der hervorragende Film revolutionierte das anspruchsvolle Lustspiel, war aber auch Chaplins einziger Misserfolg an den Kinokassen. Ausgeglichen wurde dies schnell durch den Triumph von *Goldrausch* (1925), der erneut Chaplins Überzeugung unter Beweis stellte, dass Tragödie und Komödie eng beieinander liegen: Der urkomische Film inspirierte sich an den schweren Entbehrungen der Goldsucher in den 1890er Jahren.

Die Einführung des Tonfilms 1927 war für Chaplin eine größere Herausforderung als für die meisten anderen Regisseure. Seine stumme Pantomime hatte ihm ein weltweites Publikum beschert, das durch englische Dialoge unweigerlich schrumpfen würde. Chaplin reagierte, indem er mit *Lichter der Großstadt* (1931) und *Moderne Zeiten* (1936) weiterhin Stummfilme drehte, wobei er die Tonspur ausschließlich für Toneffekte und die selbst komponierte Musikbegleitung verwendete. Damit war er nun nicht nur Produzent, Regisseur, Autor und Hauptdarsteller seiner Filme, sondern ebenfalls Komponist.

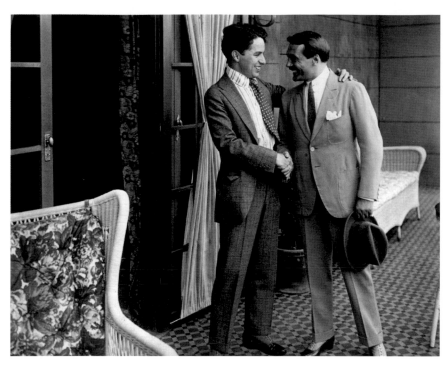

In *Moderne Zeiten* setzte Chaplin seine Komik als Waffe ein, um brennende Themen seiner Zeit anzugehen, wie die Industrialisierung oder die Konfrontation von Unternehmern und Arbeitern. In *Der große Diktator* (1940) wurden Faschismus, Nationalsozialismus und ihre jeweili-

CHAPLIN & MAX LINDER (1921)
The work of great French film comedian Max Linder influenced Chaplin. / Chaplin wurde vom Werk des französischen Filmkomikers Max Linder beeinflusst. / Chaplin fut influencé par l'œuvre de Max Linder.

gen Führer – die größten Gefahren der damaligen Zeit – zur Zielscheibe seines Spotts. Kritiker beklagten, dass der Komiker hier seine Zuständigkeiten überschritten habe.

Chaplins unablässiges Eintreten für die Unterdrückten und seine Freundschaft zu linken Intellektuellen waren der amerikanischen Rechten stets ein Dorn im Auge gewesen. Mit Beginn des Kalten Kriegs und der Kommunistenhatz durch McCarthy wurde Chaplin zu einer prominenten Zielscheibe. Der satirische Film *Monsieur Verdoux: Der Frauenmörder von Paris* (1947), der die Taten eines Massenmörders mit dem legitimierten Töten im Krieg gleichsetzt, schürte den Zorn noch. Nach *Rampenlicht* (1952), einer bittersüßen Reminiszenz an die Varietézeit seiner Jugend, kehrte er Amerika deshalb endgültig den Rücken und ließ sich dauerhaft in der Schweiz nieder. In London drehte er noch zwei weitere Filme: *Ein König in New York* (1957), eine Satire auf den politischen Verfolgungswahn in den Vereinigten Staaten, und *Die Gräfin von Hongkong* (1967). Bis zum Schluss ein unermüdlicher Arbeiter, veröffentlichte er eine zweibändige Autobiografie, komponierte Musiken für seine alten Stummfilme und plante noch einen neuen Film. Er starb am Weihnachtstag 1977.

CHARLIE CHAPLIN : LE PETIT BONHOMME

David Robinson

Plus de soixante-dix ans après sa dernière apparition à l'écran, le personnage de Charlot demeure non seulement l'un des plus grands mythes de l'histoire du cinéma, mais également une légende du vingtième siècle. Sa célèbre silhouette reste adulée et reconnue aux quatre coins du monde. Ce succès inégalé auprès d'un public universel s'explique sans doute par la capacité de Chaplin à transformer en comédie les angoisses et les difficultés fondamentales de la condition humaine, reflets de sa propre existence. Né à Londres d'artistes de music-hall qui se séparent dès son plus jeune âge, il grandit dans la misère et passe une partie de son enfance dans des pension-nats pour enfants déshérités. À dix ans, la fortune lui sourit enfin lorsqu'il fait ses débuts dans le monde du spectacle. Des emplois dans des troupes de music-hall et trois ans de théâtre lui con-fèrent très tôt une précieuse expérience de la scène. Ses talents sont affinés par un contrat de plusieurs années dans la troupe de Fred Karno, le plus brillant impresario anglais.

Lors d'une tournée aux États-Unis, il est repéré et engagé par les studios Keystone de Mack Sennett. Il comprend vite que pour imposer son style dans les comédies, il doit être son propre metteur en scène. Assimilant les techniques de tournage à une vitesse phénoménale, il ne lui faudra que trois mois avant de se mettre à réaliser tous ses films. Toujours en quête d'une plus grande indépendance et d'un meilleur salaire, il quitte Keystone pour Essanay, puis pour Mutual. Aux cours des quatre premières années, il passe des farces insouciantes tournées pour Keystone à des comédies plus ironiques et sentimentales, avant de réaliser pour Mutual des bijoux tels que *Charlot brocanteur* (1916), *Charlot policeman* (1917) et *L'Émigrant* (1917).

En 1918, grâce à un accord avec la société de distribution First National, il peut s'offrir le luxe de construire son propre studio à la pointe de la technologie de l'époque, avec sa propre écurie d'acteurs et de techniciens. Là, il transformera les horreurs de la Première Guerre mondiale en une comédie intitulée *Charlot soldat* (1918) et rappellera les privations et les angoisses de sa propre enfance dans *Le Kid* (1921), trouvant un partenaire idéal en la personne du petit Jackie Coogan, âgé de seulement cinq ans.

STILL FROM 'THE CIRCUS' (1928)
This is not a trick, and Chaplin's fear was genuine. /
Dies ist kein Trick, und Chaplins Furcht war nicht
gespielt. / Il n'y a pas de trucage et la peur de Chaplin
est bien réelle.

« [L]e génie obstiné, suspect, égocentrique,
exaspérant et adorable d'un enfant à problèmes,
Charlie Chaplin. »
Mary Pickford, 1953

CHAPLIN MEETS THE PRESS (c. 1918)
Chaplin was constantly pursued by the press. / Chaplin wurde ständig von der Presse verfolgt. / Chaplin est constamment poursuivi par la presse.

En 1919, les quatre géants de Hollywood que sont à l'époque Charlie Chaplin, Douglas Fairbanks, Mary Pickford et le réalisateur D. W. Griffith fondent United Artists (les Artistes Associés) afin de distribuer eux-mêmes leurs films. Le premier film que Chaplin produit par ce biais est *L'Opinion publique* (1923). Cette œuvre dramatique, dans laquelle il ne fait qu'une brève apparition, est destinée à mettre en valeur Edna Purviance, sa fidèle partenaire et sa maîtresse épisodique depuis 1915. Cet excellent film révolutionne le style des comédies sophistiquées ; c'est pourtant le seul désastre commercial de Chaplin. Celui-ci est compensé par le triomphe de *La Ruée vers l'or* (1925), qui démontre une nouvelle fois que chez Chaplin, le rire n'est jamais très loin des larmes. Cette comédie hilarante raconte en effet les terribles privations subies par les chercheurs d'or dans les années 1890.

L'avènement du parlant en 1927 constitue un plus grand défi pour Chaplin que pour la plupart de ses confrères. Ses pantomimes ont conquis un public universel dont il perdra inévitablement une partie s'il se met à s'exprimer en anglais. Chaplin continue donc à faire des films muets – *Les Lumières de la ville* (1931) et *Les Temps modernes* (1936) – dont la bande son ne comporte que des bruitages et un accompagnement musical. La musique est composée par Chaplin en personne, qui ajoute ainsi une nouvelle corde à son arc de scénariste, d'acteur et de réalisateur.

Dans *Les Temps modernes*, Chaplin utilise l'arme de l'humour pour dénoncer les questions brûlantes de l'époque, telles que l'industrialisation et la confrontation du capital et du travail. Dans *Le Dictateur* (1940), il prend pour cible le fascisme et ses dirigeants, qui constituent alors la principale menace. Les critiques reprocheront toutefois au comique de sortir de son rôle.

Sa constante défense des opprimés et son amitié avec des intellectuels de gauche ont toujours suscité la méfiance de la droite américaine. Avec la guerre froide et la chasse aux sorcières entreprise par les maccarthystes, Chaplin se retrouve directement en ligne de mire. *Monsieur Verdoux* (1947), film satirique qui établit un parallèle entre les forfaits d'un tueur en série et les massacres autorisés en temps de guerre, ne fait qu'aggraver son cas. Après *Les Feux de la rampe* (1952), souvenir aigre-doux de ses débuts au music-hall, Chaplin quitte l'Amérique pour s'exiler définitivement en Suisse. À Londres, il tourne encore deux films, *Un roi à New York* (1957), satire de la paranoïa du monde politique américain, et *La Comtesse de Hong-Kong* (1967). Inlassable jusqu'à la fin, il publie deux volumes autobiographiques, compose de la musique pour ses anciens films muets et prépare encore un nouveau scénario. Il meurt le jour de Noël 1977.

'DAILY MIRROR' (1952)
When Chaplin's permit to return to USA was rescinded, it made world headlines. / Als Chaplin die Genehmigung zur Wiedereinreise in die USA verweigert wurde, kam das weltweit in die Schlagzeilen. / L'annulation de son visa de retour aux États-Unis fait les gros titres dans le monde entier.

2

VISUAL FILMOGRAPHY

FILMOGRAFIE IN BILDERN
FILMOGRAPHIE EN IMAGES

KEYSTONE

1914

STILL FROM 'MAKING A LIVING' (1914)
In his first film, Chaplin is the unlikeable man who vies
with Henry Lehrman for the love of Virginia Kirtley. /
In seinem ersten Film ist Chaplin der unsympathische
Kerl, der neben Henry Lehrman um die Gunst von
Virginia Kirtley buhlt. / Dans son premier film, Chaplin
est un personnage peu sympathique qui tente de ravir
Virginia Kirtley à son rival Henry Lehrman.

PAGE 22
**PORTRAIT FROM 'A NIGHT IN A LONDON
CLUB' (1910)**
Chaplin specialised in inebriate characters when
performing with the Karno vaudeville company. /
Bei seinen Auftritten mit der Karno-Varietétruppe
war Chaplin auf die Darstellung von Trunkenbolden
spezialisiert. / Lorsqu'il se produit avec la troupe de
vaudeville de Karno, Chaplin se spécialise dans les
personnages éméchés.

STILL FROM 'MAKING A LIVING' (1914)
Henry Lehrman (center) was also the director, and he
made a slapstick comedy in the standard Keystone
manner. According to Chaplin, Lehrman cut out a lot of
his funny business. / Henry Lehrman (Mitte) war auch
der Regisseur und drehte eine Slapstick-Komödie nach
altbekannter Keystone-Manier. Chaplin zufolge schnitt
Lehrman viele seiner komischen Einlagen heraus. /
Henry Lehrman (au centre), également réalisateur,
tourne une comédie burlesque dans le plus pur style
Keystone. Selon Chaplin, il coupera beaucoup de ses
passages comiques.

PAGES 26 & 27
**STILLS FROM 'KID AUTO RACES AT VENICE'
(1914)**
The debut of the iconic costume. Chaplin plays a man
who persistently stands in front of the camera, much to
the annoyance of the director. The whole thing was
filmed in 45 minutes. / Das Debüt des legendären
Kostüms. Chaplin spielt einen Mann, der ständig vor der
Kamera steht – sehr zum Ärger des Regisseurs. Das
Ganze wurde in einer Dreiviertelstunde abgedreht. /
Les débuts de son légendaire costume. Chaplin incarne
un homme qui se place constamment devant l'objectif,
au grand dam du réalisateur. Le tournage est achevé en
45 minutes.

AUTO RACES AT VENICE CAL

IN PICTURING THIS EVENT AN
ODD CHARACTER DISCOVERED
THAT MOTION PICTURES WERE
BEING TAKEN AND IT BECAME
IMPOSSIBLE TO KEEP HIM
AWAY FROM THE CAMERA

The first sub-title (from a genuine
Keystone Print)

Chaplin at first obstructs the view of the
The starting-point

which is taking Press photographs
and strikes a pose

requests for his departure

middle of the course, but soon returns to the camera. Persuasion

But Chaplin picks up his hat and returns to face the

in at first obstructs the view of the crowd   then gets in front of the camera

produce a different pose.   He goes off for a stroll in the

, the cameraman resorts to force.

in even more striking poses   and at shorter range

STILL FROM 'MABEL'S STRANGE PREDICAMENT' (1914)
This film, with Mabel Normand (a much bigger star at the time), was made the week before 'Kid Auto Races at Venice' and so is actually the first time Chaplin wore the tramp costume. / Dieser Film mit Mabel Normand, die damals ein viel größerer Star war, entstand in der Woche vor *Kid Auto Races at Venice.* Hier trug Chaplin das erste Mal sein Tramp-Kostüm. / Ce film avec Mabel Normand (une star de l'époque) est tourné une semaine avant *Charlot est content de lui.* C'est donc le premier où apparaît le costume de Charlot.

"There was a cabstand nearby and an old character they called "Rummy" Binks was one of the landmarks... When I saw Rummy shuffle his way across the pavement to hold a cabman's horse for a penny tip, I was fascinated. The walk was so funny to me that I imitated it... Day after day I cultivated that walk. It became an obsession. Whenever I pulled it, I was sure of a laugh. Now, no matter what else I may do that is amusing, I can never get away from the walk."
Charles Chaplin, 'McClure's Magazine' (1916)

STILL FROM 'BETWEEN SHOWERS' (1914)
There were several standard set-ups for a Keystone comedy. One was to move the actors to a park and have two characters (Chaplin and Ford Sterling) fight for a sweetheart (Emma Clifton) until a police officer (Chester Conklin) is needed to keep the peace. / Es gab verschiedene Standardeinstellungen für eine Keystone-Komödie. Eine davon bestand darin, zwei Figuren (Chaplin und Ford Sterling) in einem Park um ihr Herzblatt (Emma Clifton) kämpfen zu lassen, bis ein Ordnungshüter (Chester Conklin) einschreiten muss, um den Frieden wiederherzustellen. / L'une des intrigues standard des comédies Keystone : dans un parc, deux personnages (Chaplin et Ford Sterling) se battent pour l'amour d'une belle (Emma Clifton) jusqu'à ce qu'un policier (Chester Conklin) vienne rétablir l'ordre.

PAGES 30 & 31
STILLS FROM 'A FILM JOHNNIE' (1914)
Chaplin gets so involved in the film that the emotions on the screen become his emotions. This shows an instinctive understanding of the emotional transactions between film and the viewer. The emotions become real. / Chaplin steigert sich so sehr in die Filmhandlung hinein, dass er sich die Gefühle auf der Leinwand zu Eigen macht. Damit beweist er ein instinktives Verständnis für das Wechselspiel der Emotionen zwischen Film und Zuschauer: Gespielte Gefühle werden real. / Chaplin s'implique tellement dans le film qu'il fait siennes les émotions qu'il exprime à l'écran, comprenant instinctivement le phénomène d'identification du spectateur.

Chaplin is a too emotional cinema-goer.
He weeps at scenes of defeat — —

gets up and cheers at victories —

In consequence he is thrown out but
an ambition to join the Keystone Company

now possesses him. He waylays mem
of the company on their arrival at the S

Chaplin contrives to gain admission to the Studio   and   m

...n hardly keep his hands off the ...reen villain—

and responds ardently to the gestures of the Keystone Girl (Peggy Pearce).

...d mournfully compares his own girth ...ith that of Roscoe Arbuckle.

Arbuckle proves to have a large heart (also).

...tour of inspection.

STILL FROM 'A BUSY DAY' (1914)
Chaplin dresses as a woman to play a shrewish wife.
This comedy was made in a day, which was not unusual
for a Keystone film, so that they could shoot at a
military parade. / Chaplin verkleidet sich als
Schreckschraube. Um während einer Militärparade
filmen zu können, wurde diese Komödie an einem
einzigen Tag gedreht. Das war für einen Keystone-Film
nicht ungewöhnlich. / Chaplin travesti en mégère.
Comme souvent chez Keystone, cette comédie est
tournée en une journée, à l'occasion d'une parade
militaire.

„In der Nähe war ein Droschkenplatz, und ein altes
Original namens Rummy Binks gehörte zum
Inventar ... Wenn ich Rummy über das Pflaster
schlurfen sah, um für ein Trinkgeld von einem
Penny das Pferd eines Kutschers zu halten, dann
war ich fasziniert. Sein Gang war so komisch, dass
ich ihn nachahmte ... Jeden Tag übte ich diesen
Gang. Ich war wie besessen davon. Jedes Mal,
wenn ich ihn vorführte, waren mir die Lacher
gewiss. Und jetzt kann ich machen, was ich will, so
lustig es auch sein mag – den Gang werde ich nicht
mehr los."
Charles Chaplin, *McClure's Magazine* **(1916)**

STILL FROM 'THE FACE ON THE BAR ROOM FLOOR' (1914)

A parody of then in-vogue love poem by Hugh Antoine d'Arcy. It is directed by Chaplin, who was slowly but surely gaining control of every aspect of his work. / Eine Parodie auf ein damals sehr bekanntes Liebesgedicht von Hugh Antoine d'Arcy. Regie führte Chaplin, der allmählich die Kontrolle über sämtliche Aspekte seiner Arbeit übernahm. / Parodie d'un poème d'amour de Hugh Antoine d'Arcy en vogue à l'époque. Ce film est réalisé par Chaplin, qui prend peu à peu le contrôle de ses œuvres.

« Il y avait non loin de là une station de fiacres dont l'une des curiosités était un vieux personnage surnommé « Rummy » Binks… Quand je le voyais traverser la rue en traînant les pieds pour tenir le cheval d'un cocher contre une petite pièce, j'étais fasciné. Sa démarche me paraissait tellement drôle que je l'imitais… Jour après jour, je cultivais cette démarche. C'était devenu une obsession. Chaque fois que je l'imitais, j'étais sûr de provoquer l'hilarité. Même si je fais aujourd'hui d'autres choses amusantes, je ne pourrai jamais échapper à cette démarche. »
Charles Chaplin, *McClure's Magazine* (1916)

Shortly afterwards an unknown star appears at the Studio gates.

Her arrival creates general exc

He presses a contract on her,   and also his attentions.

and Chaplin stands revealed. The whole staff chases him, a

which is shared by the Production Manager.

Left alone for a moment the new Star disrobes,

he has to take refuge in a well.

"Chaplin is vulgar... There is vulgarity in the comedies of Aristophanes, and in those of Plautus and Terence and the Elizabethans, not excluding Shakespeare. Rabelais is vulgar, Fielding and Smollett and Swift are vulgar. Among the great comedians there is vulgarity without end. Vulgarity and distinguished art can exist together."
Minnie Maddern Fiske, American actress, 1917

„Chaplin ist vulgär ... In den Komödien des Aristophanes gibt es Vulgarität und in denen von Plautus und Terenz und bei den Elisabethanern, einschließlich Shakespeare. Rabelais ist vulgär, Fielding und Smollett und Swift sind vulgär. Unter den größten Komödianten gibt es Vulgarität ohne Ende. Vulgarität und bedeutende Kunst können nebeneinander bestehen."
Minnie Maddern Fiske, amerikanische Schauspielerin, 1917

« Chaplin est vulgaire... Il y a de la vulgarité dans les comédies d'Aristophane, tout comme dans celles de Plaute, de Térence et des Élisabéthains, Shakespeare compris. Rabelais est vulgaire, Fielding, Smollett et Swift sont vulgaires. Chez les grands comiques, il y a une vulgarité sans fin. La vulgarité et le raffinement peuvent coexister dans l'art. »
Minnie Maddern Fiske, actrice américaine, 1917

STILLS FROM 'THE MASQUERADER' (1914)
The tramp disguises himself as a film star to gain access to Keystone's film studio. / Der Tramp verkleidet sich als Filmstar, um Zutritt zum Keystone-Filmstudio zu erlangen. / Charlot se déguise en star de cinéma pour pénétrer dans les studios de Keystone.

STILL FROM 'THE ROUNDERS' (1914)
Chaplin and the famous comedian Roscoe "Fatty"
Arbuckle are drunks who attempt to sleep in a sinking
boat. / Chaplin und der berühmte Komiker Roscoe
„Fatty" Arbuckle spielen Betrunkene, die in einem
sinkenden Boot zu schlafen versuchen. / Chaplin et le
célèbre comique Roscoe (alias Fatty) Arbuckle en
ivrognes tentant de trouver le sommeil dans un bateau
en train de couler.

STILL FROM 'GENTLEMEN OF NERVE' (1914)
This improvised film at a racetrack shows that the
crowd already know Charlie, and that he is becoming
famous. / Der auf einer Rennbahn improvisierte Film
belegt, dass das Publikum Charlie bereits kannte und
dass er auf dem Weg zum Ruhm war. / Cette scène
improvisée sur un champ de courses montre la célébrité
naissante de Charlot auprès des badauds.

PAGES 38 & 39
STILLS FROM 'HIS PREHISTORIC PAST' (1914)
Chaplin tried out many ideas that he used with greater
finesse in later films. Here the tramp is brought back to
reality just in time. / Chaplin probierte viele Ideen aus,
die er in späteren Filmen mit größerer Finesse
umsetzte. Hier findet der Tramp gerade noch
rechtzeitig zurück in die Wirklichkeit. / Chaplin
expérimente de nombreuses idées qu'il réutilisera par
la suite. Ici, Charlot se réveille juste à temps.

PAGES 40/41
CINEMA (1915)
Chaplin had won worldwide fame in just one year. /
In nur einem Jahr war Chaplin weltberühmt geworden. /
Chaplin s'est forgé une notoriété mondiale en un an
seulement.

Swain is presumed dead and Chaplin

His popularity is interfered with by a riva

and by a stray arrow. Meanwhile Swain has reco
and vows vengeance,

16

omes a popular hero.

20

for a short time only. But his courtship is disturbed by the incoming tide

24

which he soon performs. Chaplin is awakened by cramp.

"I have stuck to comedy because I am convinced that my public is better satisfied with that than with any other kind of production. I essayed the 'straight drama' once or twice, and cannot say that my efforts in that direction were very highly appreciated."
Charles Chaplin, 'The Strand Magazine' (January 1918)

„Ich bin bei der Komödie geblieben, weil ich davon überzeugt bin, dass mein Publikum damit besser zufriedengestellt wird als mit jeder anderen Art von Film. Ich habe mich ein- oder zweimal an ‚normalen Dramen' versucht und kann nicht behaupten, dass meine Vorstöße in diese Richtung besonders hohe Wertschätzung erfahren hätten."
Charles Chaplin, The Strand Magazine (Januar 1918)

« Je m'en suis tenu à la comédie parce que je suis convaincu que c'est ce qui plaît le plus à mon public. Je me suis essayé une fois ou deux au "drame classique", mais je ne peux pas dire que mes efforts en ce sens aient été très appréciés. »
Charles Chaplin, The Strand Magazine (janvier 1918)

Tillie loses all self-restraint and

The Keystone Cops

into the sea,

STILLS FROM 'TILLIE'S PUNCTURED ROMANCE' (1914)
The first feature-length slapstick film had stage star Marie Dressler supported by film stars Chaplin and Mabel Normand. / Im ersten abendfüllenden Slapstickfilm spielte Theaterstar Marie Dressler die Hauptrolle, unterstützt von den Filmstars Chaplin und Mabel Normand. / Le premier long métrage burlesque est interprété par la comédienne de théâtre Marie Dressler, entourée des vedettes de cinéma Charlie Chaplin et Mabel Normand.

sues Chaplin & Mabel with a revolver on to a jetty.

called out. Their erratic driving pushes Tillie

d their car follows. Mabel & Chaplin watch with horror,

ESSANAY

1915–1916

STILL FROM 'HIS NEW JOB' (1915)
With cross-eyed comedian Ben Turpin. / Mit dem
schielenden Komiker Ben Turpin. / Avec le comédien
bigleux Ben Turpin.

PAGE 44
**PORTRAIT FROM 'CHARLIE CHAPLIN'S
BURLESQUE ON CARMEN' (1916)**
As Darn Hosiery. / Als Darn Hosiery. / Dans le rôle de
Darn Hosiery.

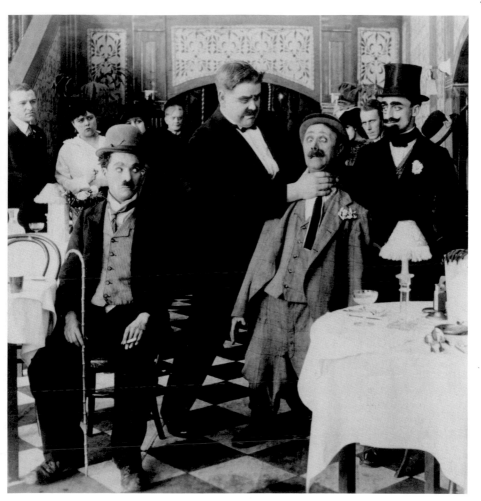

STILL FROM 'A NIGHT OUT' (1915)
Chaplin and Turpin are a pair of drunks out on the
town. / Chaplin und Turpin machen als Säufer die Stadt
unsicher. / Chaplin et Turpin incarnent deux ivrognes
partis faire la noce.

STILL FROM 'IN THE PARK' (1915)
Another 'park' film, this time with Edna Purviance
and Ernest Van Pelt. Edna remained his leading lady for
8 years. / Noch ein „Parkfilm", diesmal mit Edna
Purviance und Ernest Van Pelt. Edna war acht Jahre
lang seine Hauptdarstellerin. / Autre film tourné dans
un parc, avec Edna Purviance et Ernest Van Pelt. Edna
restera sa partenaire pendant huit ans.

PORTRAIT FROM 'THE CHAMPION' (1915)
Chaplin's first demonstration of his balletic boxing
skills. / Hier zeigt Chaplin zum ersten Mal sein
ballettartiges Boxtalent. / La première démonstration
de boxe « chorégraphiée » effectuée par Chaplin.

STILL FROM 'A JITNEY ELOPEMENT' (1915)
Chaplin tries to save his sweetheart Edna Purviance
from an arranged marriage with Leo White. / Chaplin
versucht, seine geliebte Edna vor einer Zwangsheirat
mit Leo White zu bewahren. / Chaplin tente de sauver
sa bien-aimée (Edna Purviance) d'un mariage arrangé
avec Leo White.

STILL FROM 'THE TRAMP' (1915)
Chaplin gradually changed the Tramp to tone down his
obnoxious characteristics and to add more sentiment. /
Chaplin veränderte den Tramp allmählich, indem er
seine unangenehmen Charaktereigenschaften
zurücknahm und ihm mehr Gefühl verlieh. / Chaplin fait
progressivement évoluer le personnage de Charlot,
atténuant ses côtés odieux pour le rendre plus
sentimental.

STILL FROM 'BY THE SEA' (1915)
A romantic moment improvised by the Venice,
California amusement pier. / Ein romantischer
Augenblick wird am Vergnügungspier von Venice in
Kalifornien improvisiert. / Scène romantique improvisée
à Venice, en Californie.

STILL FROM 'WORK' (1915)
This film shows Chaplin's wakening social conscience as he uses comedy to criticize the exploitation of workers. / Dieser Film bezeugt das Erwachen von Chaplins sozialem Gewissen: Er bedient sich der Komödie, um die Ausbeutung der Arbeiter anzuprangern. / Ce film montre l'éveil de la conscience sociale de Chaplin, qui dénonce l'exploitation des travailleurs par le biais de la comédie.

PAGE 54
COMIC STRIP: 'THE FUNNY WONDER' (1915)
Chaplin's iconic image was often used without his knowledge and without payment. / Chaplins unverkennbare Figur wurde oft ohne sein Wissen benutzt – und ohne dass er Tantiemen erhielt. / La figure légendaire de Charlot est souvent utilisée sans autorisation ni rétribution.

PAGE 55
COVER OF 'THE FAMILY JOURNAL' (1915)
In 1915 worldwide press interest in Chaplin was dubbed "Chaplinitis."/ Im Jahre 1915 bezeichnete man das weltweite Interesse an Charlie als „Chaplinitis". / En 1915, l'engouement de la presse internationale pour Chaplin est qualifié de « Chaplinite ».

CHARLIE CHAPLIN APPEARS TO-DAY. CHARLIE CHAPLIN

The Funny Wonder ½

VOL. II.—No. 72.] EVERY TUESDAY. [WEEK ENDING AUGUST 7, 1915.

CHARLIE CHAPLIN, the Scream of the Earth (*the famous Essanay Comedian*).

1. Here he 'ia, readers! Good old Charlie! Absolutely IT! A scream from start to finish. What's he doing now, eh? "'Twas here," says he, standing in a graceful posish, by an artistically designed coal-hole, with the faithful hound attached to his cane: "'Twas here I was to meet Maggie Phwpats!" But see! A rival approaches!

2. Then the rival, one Esmond MacSydeslyppe Hugo Balscadden O'Chuckilupp—the rival, we repeat, did a bit of dirty work. Fact! He held forth a tempting bone, and Charlie's faithful hound cast the eye of approval on same. Bazz rival! "Soon," says the chirpy Charlie, putting on another fag: "Soon she will be here. Oh, joy!"

3. But the hound, deciding to do the chew on the bone, legged it up the paving stones, taking Charlie's stick with him. And Charlie, with his visible means of support thus removed, did a graceful flop into said coal-hole just as the lovely Maggie appeared! "Charlie!" said she, with much spurnery, "What do you think you're doing?"

4. Ha! Enter the rival! "Don't you have anything to do with him, Maggie," says the rival; "He's absolutely sale price, he is. Marked down to one-and-nine-three-him! Come with me to some nook, where we may hold converse!"

5. So off they went to the nook, but Charlie was soon up and doing. Yea! He flopped along, soon coming upon the rival telling the tale of love to the beauteous one. "Ho!" says he. "Now to get a portion of my own back! Now for it!"

6. Well, the rival was just on the point of laying his riches at the damsel's dainty patent number two's, when Charlie, picking up a dustbin (full flavour) which happened to be handy, shoved it into his outstretched fins. Which did it—yes!

7. Up jumped the young person. Talk about the frozen eye! she said; "I did not come here to be entertained by such poltroonery. Your face causes me uneasiness! No explanations, please! Get hence and proceed forthwith. All is over between us!" Or words to that effect. Then Charlie did the inward chuckle, and raised his hat with courtly grace.

8. And he did the affable and endearing chat that completely restored him to favour in the damsel's eyes. "Permit me to suggest," says this gallant old filbert, "a light lunch at the Café de Chabcritt, with a jaunt on the merry old motor-'bus to follow. Having just received my quarterly allowance—not half—all is well. Let us proceed!" And they did proceed—some! More news next week, so look out!

THE Family Journal
A WEEKLY PAPER FOR THE HOUSEHOLD
PRICE 1D. EVERY WEDNESDAY

Charlie's Lucky
HORSE-SHOE
AND THE
Charlie Chaplin
CHARM
OFFERED TO READERS
FREE!

£40
in Cash Prizes
EVERY WEEK!
SEE
'Topical Tales'
Competition inside.

CHARLIE CHAPLIN
APPEARS IN
THIS NUMBER

The Champion Mirth-Maker IN YOUR Own Home!
SEE PAGE 509.

PORTRAIT FROM 'A WOMAN' (1915)
Chaplin's most accomplished female impersonation. /
Chaplin als Frauendarsteller in Vollendung. / Chaplin
dans son rôle de femme le plus accompli.

STILL FROM 'THE BANK' (1915)
The bank janitor's gallantry is selective. The sad ending
was a first for film comedy and anticipates his later
style. / Der Hausmeister der Bank behandelt nicht alle
gleich zuvorkommend. Der traurige Schluss war in der
Filmkomödie etwas Neues und nahm Chaplins späteren
Stil vorweg. / Un portier à la galanterie sélective. Le
triste dénouement du film, une première dans l'histoire
de la comédie, annonce le style ultérieur de Chaplin.

STILL FROM 'A NIGHT IN THE SHOW' (1915)
Chaplin plays dual roles in this adaptation of his Fred
Karno sketch 'Mumming Birds.' / Chaplin hat eine
Doppelrolle in der Verfilmung seines Fred-Karno-
Sketchs *Mumming Birds*. / Chaplin interprète des
doubles rôles dans cette adaptation de *Mumming Birds*,
le sketch qu'il interprétait chez Fred Karno.

STILL FROM 'SHANGHAIED' (1915)
Charlie is hired to shanghai a crew but is himself
shanghaied. His hand gesture is one that reoccurs
throughout his career. / Charlie wird angeheuert, um
eine Mannschaft zu schanghaien, wird aber selbst
schanghait. Die Handgeste benutzt er während seiner
gesamten Karriere immer wieder. / Embauché pour
embarquer un équipage, Charlot se retrouve lui-même
embarqué. Son geste de la main reviendra tout au long
de sa carrière.

STILL FROM 'POLICE' (1916)
When Charlie gets out of jail, he and his former cellmate (hidden behind Charlie) decide to rob Edna Purviance's house. / Nach Charlies Entlassung aus dem Gefängnis will er mit seinem ehemaligen Zellengenossen (hinter Charlie versteckt) das Haus von Edna Purviance ausrauben. / À sa sortie de prison, Charlot décide de cambrioler la maison d'Edna Purviance avec son ancien compagnon de cellule (caché derrière lui).

PORTRAIT FROM 'CHARLIE CHAPLIN'S BURLESQUE ON CARMEN' (1916)
Then as now, it was common for comedies to parody contemporary hits, in this case Cecil B. DeMille's 'Carmen.' / Damals wie heute parodieren Komödien häufig aktuelle Hits – in diesem Fall Cecil B. DeMilles Carmen. / Les comédies de l'époque parodient déjà fréquemment des succès contemporains, en l'occurrence Carmen de Cecil B. DeMille.

MUTUAL

1916–1917

ON THE SET OF 'THE FLOORWALKER' (1916)
Another year, another bigger contract. Chaplin received
$10,000 a week and the Lone Star studio to play with.
At that time sets were built on an open-air stage with
muslin overhead to diffuse the sunlight. Here Chaplin is
planning 'The Floorwalker.' / Ein Jahr später folgte
ein noch lukrativerer Vertrag. Chaplin verdiente
10.000 Dollar in der Woche und konnte sich im Lone-
Star-Studio nach Herzenslust austoben. Damals wurden
die Bühnenbilder im Freien aufgebaut und mit Musselin
abgedeckt, um das Sonnenlicht zu zerstreuen. Hier
plant Chaplin gerade *Der Ladenaufseher*. / Chaque
année apporte un nouveau contrat plus juteux. Chaplin
obtient 10 000 dollars par semaine et de nouveaux
studios. Les décors construits en plein air sont
surmontés de mousseline pour diffuser la lumière du
soleil. Ici, Chaplin prévoit de tourner *Charlot chef de
rayon*.

PAGE 62
STILL FROM 'THE ADVENTURER' (1917)
"The Eel" (Chaplin) is right under the nose of the
prison guard (Frank J. Coleman). / Der „Aal"
(Chaplin) steckt direkt unter dem Gefängniswärter
Frank J. Coleman. / « L'Anguille » (Chaplin) sous le
nez du gardien de prison (Frank J. Coleman).

STILL FROM 'THE FLOORWALKER' (1916)
A slapstick moment in this comedy of embezzlement
and switched identities. / Ein Slapstick-Moment in der
Unterschlagungs- und Verwechslungskomödie. / Scène
burlesque dans une histoire de détournement de fonds
et d'usurpation d'identité.

*"From the making of pictures I get a good deal of
thrill. I get it more as a director and producer than
I do as an actor. It is the old satisfaction that
someone is making something, forming something
that has body."*
Charles Chaplin, 'Adelphi Magazine' (January 1925)

*„Das Filmemachen erzeugt bei mir einen
ordentlichen Nervenkitzel, und zwar als Regisseur
und Produzent mehr als in der Funktion des
Schauspielers. Es ist die uralte Befriedigung, etwas
zu schaffen, etwas zu formen, das Substanz hat."*
Charles Chaplin, *Adelphi Magazine* (Januar 1925)

*« Faire des films me procure une grande joie.
J'éprouve plus de bonheur comme réalisateur et
comme producteur qu'en tant qu'acteur. C'est
l'éternelle satisfaction que l'on éprouve en
fabriquant quelque chose, en façonnant un objet
qui a du corps. »*
Charles Chaplin, *Adelphi Magazine* (janvier 1925)

STILL FROM 'THE FIREMAN' (1916)
Charlie makes a daring rescue of his sweetheart Edna. /
Charlie bei einer verwegenen Rettungsaktion für seine
geliebte Edna. / Charlot entreprend le sauvetage
périlleux de sa bien-aimée, Edna.

STILL FROM 'THE FIREMAN' (1916)
Eric Campbell and Charlie try to control the hose. /
Eric Campbell und Charlie versuchen, den Schlauch zu
bändigen. / Eric Campbell et Charlot aux prises avec un
tuyau récalcitrant.

STILL FROM 'THE VAGABOND' (1916)
Eric Campbell, Chaplin's best villain, dispatches Charlie
and menaces Edna. / Chaplins bester Bösewicht Eric
Campbell räumt Charlie aus dem Weg und bedroht
Edna. / Eric Campbell, le « méchant » le plus réussi de
Chaplin, expédie Charlot et menace Edna.

*"Action is more generally understood than words.
The lift of an eyebrow, however faint, may convey
more than a hundred words."*
Charles Chaplin, 'The New York Times' (25 January 1931)

„Handlung wird allgemein besser verstanden als Worte. Das Zucken einer Augenbraue, und sei es noch so unscheinbar, kann mehr ausdrücken als hundert Worte."
Charles Chaplin, *The New York Times* (25. Januar 1931)

« On comprend généralement mieux les gestes que les paroles. Un sourcil qui se lève, même imperceptiblement, en dit plus long qu'une centaine de mots. »
Charles Chaplin, *The New York Times* (25 janvier 1931)

STILL FROM 'ONE A.M.' (1916)
In a virtuoso performance, Chaplin plays a drunk who arrives home and tries to go to bed, but every object in the house prevents him from achieving his aim. /
In einer virtuosen Darbietung spielt Chaplin einen Betrunkenen, der nach Hause kommt und versucht, zu Bett zu gehen. Doch alle Gegenstände im Haus hindern ihn an seinem Vorhaben. / Dans un numéro de virtuose, Chaplin incarne un ivrogne qui tente d'aller se coucher tandis que les objets semblent se liguer contre lui.

STILL FROM 'THE COUNT' (1916)
Charlie masquerades as a count at a fancy-dress party,
allowing him to work with one of his favourite themes:
the contrasts between rich and poor. / Charlie
verkleidet sich auf einer Kostümparty als Graf. Hier
kann Chaplin wieder einmal eines seiner
Lieblingsthemen aufgreifen: den Gegensatz zwischen
Arm und Reich. / Déguisé en comte dans un bal
costumé, Chaplin explore l'un de ses thèmes favoris :
le contraste entre les classes sociales.

STILL FROM 'THE PAWNSHOP' (1916)
A broom becomes a cue. Much of Chaplin's comedy
came from changing the use of objects. / Ein Besen wird
zum Queue: Chaplins Komik entstand häufig aus der
Zweckentfremdung von Gegenständen. / Un balai se
transforme en queue de billard. Chaplin tire souvent
ses effets comiques de l'utilisation des objets à contre-
emploi.

STILL FROM 'BEHIND THE SCREEN' (1916)
Edna Purviance disguises herself as a boy to gain entry
into a film studio, where Chaplin works as a property
boy. / Edna Purviance verkleidet sich als Junge, um in
ein Filmstudio hineinzugelangen, in dem Chaplin als
Requisiteur arbeitet. / Edna Purviance se travestit en
garçon pour accéder à un studio de cinéma où Chaplin
travaille comme accessoiriste.

STILL FROM 'THE RINK' (1916)
Chaplin developed his balletic rollerskating skills for the
Fred Karno sketch 'Skating.' / Chaplin entwickelte das
ballettartige Rollschuhlaufen für den Fred-Karno-
Sketch *Skating*. / Chaplin a appris à patiner avec des
grâces de ballerine pour le sketch de Fred Karno
intitulé *Skating*.

STILL FROM 'THE CURE' (1917)
A massage metamorphs into a wrestling bout. / Eine
Massage weitet sich zum Ringkampf aus. / Une séance
de massage qui tourne au combat de catch.

STILL FROM 'EASY STREET' (1917)
The local criminals fear Charlie after he bests bully Eric
Campbell. Chaplin based the T-junction street set on his
childhood memories of South London. / Die kleinen
Gauner fürchten sich vor Charlie, nachdem er den
gefürchteten Schläger Eric Campbell besiegt hat. Die
T-förmige Straßeneinmündung entstammte Chaplins
Süd-Londoner Kindheitserinnerungen und kam noch in
vielen weiteren Filmen vor. / La pègre locale se met à
redouter Charlot, qui a battu le caïd Eric Campbell. Ce
carrefour inspiré des souvenirs d'enfance de Chaplin à
Londres sera présent dans de nombreux films.

ON THE SET OF 'THE IMMIGRANT' (1917)
Chaplin with protective older brother Sydney, who was
a comedian and writer. They retained a close
relationship throughout their lives. / Chaplin mit seinem
älteren Bruder und Beschützer Sydney, der Komiker
und Schriftsteller war. Sie hatten ein Leben lang ein
sehr inniges Verhältnis. / Chaplin avec son frère aîné
Sydney, comédien et écrivain. Ils demeureront proches
tout au long de leur vie.

HITTIER HERALD

EVENING EDITION ONE CENT

FRIDAY, AUGUST 3, 1917 — Weather: Fair, Slightly Cooler.

$19,530,000 GOLD AMERICA PAID OUT NOW COMES BACK

Brought Here From Halifax, It Will Settle Through J. P. Morgan & Co. War Debts Contracted by Great Britain.

ABOUT $25,000,000 IN SECURITIES ALSO ARRIVE.

Guarded Treasure Is Carted Through Streets to Sub-Treasury and There Checked Up.

American gold coin to the amount of $19,530,000, which had been shipped to England in years of trade indebtedness by this country to England and lodged in the vaults of the Bank of England, was taken into the Sub-Treasury in this city yesterday and placed to the credit of J. P. Morgan & Co., so that Great Britain may pay part of its large and growing indebtedness to manufacturers and producers in this country.

A block of securities was brought with the gold. These also were conreceiving bankers refused to talk about the amount, source or disposition of the stocks or bonds. Guesses accompanying the special train all the way from Halifax agreed that the securities were worth $25,000,000. On

CRIMINAL ESCAPES
CONVICT AT LARGE

Officials Completely Baffled

Rain of Bullets Fail to Stop Convict No. 23 in Wild Dash from State Prison.

The most daring escape in the history of the State Prison was that today of Convict No. 23, known to the authorities as "The Eel," who gained his freedom after a mad dash through a shower of bullets and who had up to a late hour successfully covered every trace of his whereabouts.

A nation-wide alarm has been sounded, and every avenue of escape from the city is being closely watched by armed guards. Orders to return the fugitive dead or alive have been issued by the police authorities.

Already an investigation has been started by the Prison Board in an effort to determine who is to blame for this most recent outrage, and it is rumored that several of the high officials of the institution will be interrogated.

The stage at one time or another has dealt with every kind of sinner in the whole category of crime, but Saturday night at the Astor Theatre was the first instance, so far as one recalls, in which it has taken up the case of the juvenile delinquent. "Young America," by Fred Ballard, who acknowledges that the idea was suggested by certain printed stories, was written for no other purpose than to show the procedure of a children's court. As such it is a sort of

for staging the battle in which four of the fastest men in the world will compete, and which will have a day set apart all to itself, would not be decided upon until after the arrival of Bundy and would partially depend on the position which McLoughlin occupied in the singles at that time. R. Norris Williams 2d and McLoughlin, the Damon and Pythias of the courts, came in from Southampton, L. I., in the speedy little motor car in which Williams tours from tournament to tournament. The intimacy between Williams, the national champion who wrested the laurels

CONVICT No. 23, "THE EEL."

STILL FROM 'THE ADVENTURER' (1917)
The newspaper that reveals Commodore Slick to be "The Eel." / Die Zeitung deckt auf, dass Kommodore Slick der „Aal" ist. / Le journal qui révèle que « l'Anguille » n'est autre que Commodore Slick.

FIRST NATIONAL

1918–1923

PAGE 78
STILL FROM 'THE KID' (1921)
The iconic image, with the Kid (Jackie Coogan) and the cop (Tom Wilson). / Das klassische Bild mit Kind (Jackie Coogan) und Polizist (Tom Wilson). / L'image mythique du Kid (Jackie Coogan) et du policier (Tom Wilson).

THE CHAPLIN STUDIO (c. 1920)
This aerial view shows the Chaplin studio amidst orange groves. / Die Luftaufnahme zeigt das Chaplin-Studio zwischen Orangenhainen. / Vue aérienne montrant le studio Chaplin au milieu d'orangeraies.

THE CHAPLIN STUDIO BEING BUILT (1918)
Chaplin atop the skeletal framework of his new studio. / Chaplin auf dem Gerüst seines neuen Studios. / Chaplin domine la charpente de son nouveau studio.

STILL FROM 'HOW TO MAKE MOVIES' (1918)
Kevin Brownlow and David Gill edited together a
version of this abandoned film, in which Chaplin
showed how he made his pictures. In this sequence,
Chaplin works with Henry Bergman and Edna, whilst
Tom Wilson and Loyal Underwood watch at left, and
cameraman Jack Wilson is standing behind Chaplin. /
Kevin Brownlow und David Gill erstellten eine
Fassung des nicht fertig gestellten Films, in dem
Chaplin zeigte, wie er seine Filme drehte. In dieser
Szene arbeitet Chaplin mit Henry Bergman und
Edna, während links Tom Wilson und Loyal
Underwood zuschauen. Hinter Chaplin steht der
Kameramann Jack Wilson. / Projet de film avorté,
monté par Kevin Brownlow et David Gill, où Chaplin
présente ses méthodes de travail. Il travaille ici avec
Henry Bergman et Edna Purviance sous le regard de
Tom Wilson et Loyal Underwood (à gauche) et du
cameraman Jack Wilson (derrière Chaplin).

PORTRAIT FROM 'A DOG'S LIFE' (1918)
Chaplin drew a parallel between the life of the tramp,
the life of a girl in a dance hall and the life of a mongrel
dog. All of them were living "a dog's life." / Chaplin zog
Parallelen zwischen einem Landstreicher, einem
Mädchen in einem Tanzsaal und einer
Promenadenmischung. Sie alle lebten ein
„Hundeleben". / Chaplin trace un parallèle entre
l'existence d'un clochard, celle d'une chanteuse de
cabaret et celle d'un chien errant. Tous mènent
« une vie de chien ».

CHARLIE CHAPLIN SELLING BONDS (1918)
Chaplin also contributed to US war effort by speaking at bond-selling rallies. He took his speeches seriously and sold millions of dollars worth of bonds. / Chaplin unterstützte die USA im Krieg auch, indem er bei Werbeveranstaltungen zum Verkauf von Kriegsanleihen Reden hielt. Er nahm die Sache sehr ernst und „verkaufte" auf diese Weise Anleihen in Millionenhöhe. / Chaplin contribue à l'effort de guerre américain en intervenant lors de meetings en faveur des Liberty Bonds. Prenant ses discours très au sérieux, il parvient à faire vendre des millions de dollars d'obligations.

STILL FROM 'THE BOND' (1918)
The tramp smites the Kaiser (Sydney Chaplin) with a mallet representing Liberty Bonds. / Der Tramp zieht dem Kaiser (Sydney Chaplin) eins mit dem Holzhammer über. Dieser steht für die „Freiheitsanleihen" (amerikanische Kriegsanleihen). / Charlot assomme le Kaiser (Sydney Chaplin) avec un maillet représentant les « Liberty Bonds » (obligations émises pendant la guerre).

PAGES 86 & 87
POSTCARDS (c. 1918)

THE KNUTS THINK THEY'LL GET OFF QUICKER IF THEY SWANK THEY'RE CHARLIE.

I'M FOR THE FRONT

STILL FROM 'SHOULDER ARMS' (1918)
Even though he made a comedy, many of the details of
trench life were more realistic than dramatic films of
the period. / Obwohl er eine Komödie drehte, stellte er
viele Einzelheiten des Lebens in den Schützengräben
realistischer dar als „ernste" Filme der Zeit. / Bien qu'il
s'agisse d'une comédie, de nombreux détails de la vie
dans les tranchées sont plus réalistes que dans les films
dramatiques de l'époque.

STILL FROM 'SHOULDER ARMS' (1918)
Chaplin disguises himself as a German officer to rescue
Edna Purviance and his friend. / Chaplin verkleidet sich
als deutscher Offizier, um Edna Purviance und seinen
Freund zu retten. / Chaplin se déguise en officier
allemand pour secourir Edna Purviance.

PAGES 90/91
STILL FROM 'SUNNYSIDE' (1919)
Chaplin parodies Nijinsky's ballet 'L'Après-midi d'un
faune.' / Chaplin parodiert Nijinskys Ballett *L'Après-midi
d'un faune.* / Chaplin parodiant le ballet de Nijinski
L'Après-midi d'un faune.

ON THE SET OF 'A DAY'S PLEASURE (1919)
For one gag, a black musician playing on a boat
becomes so seasick that he turns white. Here Chaplin
helps apply the make-up. / Bei einem Gag wird ein
farbiger Musiker an Bord eines Schiffs so seekrank, dass
er kreidebleich wird. Hier hilft Chaplin beim Auftragen
der Maske. / Chaplin applique le maquillage pour le gag
où un musicien noir engagé sur un bateau a tellement le
mal de mer qu'il en devient blanc.

*"One of the things most quickly learned in
theatrical work is that people as a whole get
satisfaction from seeing the rich get the worst of
things. The reason for this, of course, lies in the fact
that nine tenths of the people in the world are
poor, and secretly resent the wealth of the other
tenth."*
Charles Chaplin, 'American Magazine' (1918)

STILL FROM 'THE IDLE CLASS' (1921)
Chaplin played a dual role, as tramp and alcoholic
playboy. / Chaplin spielte eine Doppelrolle als Tramp
und als alkoholsüchtiger Playboy. / Chaplin dans un
double rôle de clochard et de play-boy alcoolique.

„Eine Sache, die man am Theater sehr schnell lernt,
ist, dass die Leute insgesamt zufrieden sind, wenn
den Reichen übel mitgespielt wird. Der Grund
dafür liegt natürlich in der Tatsache, dass neun
Zehntel der Menschen auf dieser Welt arm sind
und dem restlichen Zehntel seinen Wohlstand
insgeheim übel nehmen."
Charles Chaplin, American Magazine (1918)

« L'une des choses que l'on apprend le plus vite au
théâtre, c'est que la plupart des gens se délectent
du malheur des riches. La raison est en simple :
dans le monde, neuf personnes sur dix sont
pauvres et en veulent secrètement à la dixième. »
Charles Chaplin, American Magazine (1918)

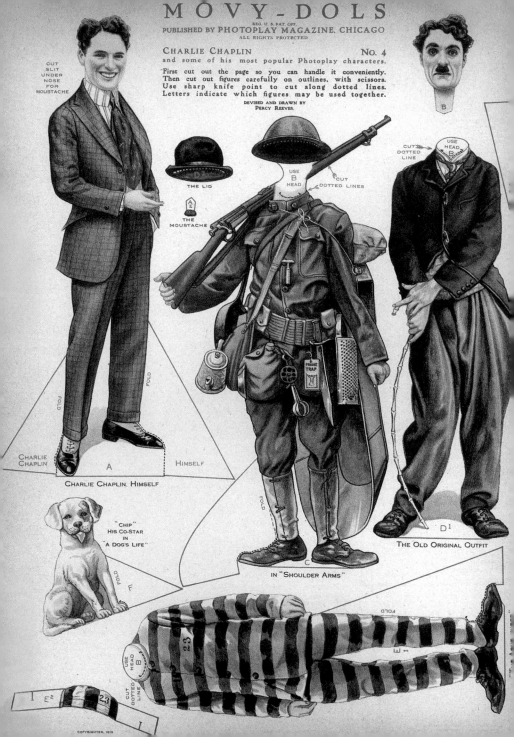

MOVY-DOLS

REG. U. S. PAT. OFF.
PUBLISHED BY PHOTOPLAY MAGAZINE, CHICAGO
ALL RIGHTS PROTECTED

CHARLIE CHAPLIN   NO. 4
and some of his most popular Photoplay characters.

First cut out the page so you can handle it conveniently.
Then cut out figures carefully on outlines, with scissors.
Use sharp knife point to cut along dotted lines.
Letters indicate which figures may be used together.

DEVISED AND DRAWN BY
PERCY REEVES.

CUT
SLIT
UNDER
NOSE
FOR
MOUSTACHE

B

THE LID

A²
THE MOUSTACHE

USE
B
HEAD

CUT
DOTTED LINES

CUT
DOTTED
LINE

USE
HEAD

FOLD

FOLD

CHARLIE
CHAPLIN

A

HIMSELF

CHARLIE CHAPLIN. HIMSELF

"CHIP"
HIS CO-STAR
IN
"A DOG'S LIFE"

FOLD

F

FOLD

PROISE
TRAP

FOLD

C

IN "SHOULDER ARMS"

D¹

THE OLD ORIGINAL OUTFIT

23

USE
HEAD
B

CUT
DOTTED
LINE

E¹

FOLD

E²

23

I

COPYRIGHTED, 1919

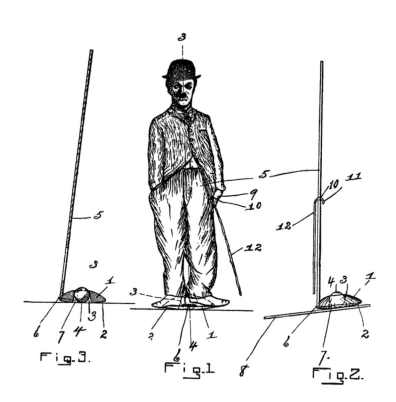

J. W. YOUNG.
TOY.
APPLICATION FILED JAN. 4, 1916.

1,209,920.

Patented Dec. 26, 1916.

PATENT FOR CHAPLIN TOY (1916)
Chaplin did not receive financial compensation for much of the merchandise that bore his image. In fact, some people complained that he earned too much money. / Chaplins Konterfei zierte viele Waren, ohne dass er finanziell beteiligt wurde. Manche meinten sogar, er verdiene ohnehin zu viel. / Beaucoup des produits à son effigie ne rapportent pas le moindre sou à Chaplin, car certains estiment qu'il gagne trop d'argent.

MOVY-DOL FROM 'PHOTOPLAY' MAGAZINE (1919)

"He is undoubtedly, a great artist; certainly he always portrays one and the same figure; only the weakly, poor, helpless, clumsy youngster for whom, however, things turn out well in the end. Now do you think that for this role he has forgotten about his own ego? On the contrary he always plays only himself as he was in his early dismal youth. He cannot get away from those impressions and to this day he obtains for himself the compensation for the frustrations and humiliations of that past period of his life."
Sigmund Freud, 1931

„Er ist unzweifelhaft ein großer Künstler, gewiß, er spielt immer nur eine und dieselbe Figur, den schwächlichen, armen, hilflosen, ungeschickten Jungen, dem es aber am Ende gut ausgeht. Nun glauben Sie, daß er für diese Rolle sein eigenes Ich vergessen muß? Im Gegenteile, er spielt immer nur sich selbst, wie er in seiner trübseligen Jugend war. Er kann von diesen Eindrücken nicht loskommen und holt sich heute noch die Entschädigungen für die Entbehrungen und Demütigungen jener Zeit."
Sigmund Freud, 1931

« C'est indéniablement un grand artiste. Certes, il dépeint toujours un seul et même personnage, le jeune homme pauvre, chétif, impuissant et maladroit qui s'en sort à la fin. Croyez-vous pour autant qu'il ait oublié son propre ego ? Au contraire, il ne fait que se représenter lui-même durant sa difficile jeunesse. Il ne peut oublier cette expérience et compense ainsi les frustrations et les humiliations de cette période de sa vie. »
Sigmund Freud, 1931

STILL FROM 'THE KID' (1921)
The film embodies poignant memories of Chaplin's own troubled childhood. / Der Film verarbeitet prägende Erinnerungen an Chaplins eigene schwere Kindheit. / Pour ce film, Chaplin s'inspire des souvenirs poignants qu'il a de sa propre enfance.

ON THE SET OF 'THE KID' (1921)

After the tragic death of his newborn son, Chaplin met the child performer Jackie Coogan and constructed the tale of the tramp and the abandoned child. / Nach dem tragischen Tod seines neugeborenen Sohns lernte Chaplin den Kinderschauspieler Jackie Coogan kennen und schrieb ihm die Geschichte vom Tramp und dem ausgesetzten Kind auf den Leib. / Après la mort tragique de son nouveau-né, Chaplin crée l'histoire du clochard et de l'enfant abandonné pour le jeune acteur Jackie Coogan.

ON THE SET OF 'THE KID' (1921)

Shooting Jackie Coogan's fight with the bully. / Bei den Dreharbeiten zu Jackie Coogans Kampf mit dem Schlägertypen. / Bagarre entre le Kid et le caïd.

STILL FROM 'THE KID' (1921)
Having come to love the child, the tramp is desperate to
save him from the orphanage. / Da er den Jungen
inzwischen lieb gewonnen hat, versucht der Tramp
verzweifelt, ihn vor dem Waisenhaus zu retten. / S'étant
pris d'affection pour l'enfant, Charlot fera tout pour le
sauver de l'orphelinat.

"He has turned film clowning into social satire and criticism, without losing his astonishing ability to make us laugh... Chaplin, like most genuine artists, is at heart a genial and gentle anarchist and the laughter he provokes only clears and sweetens the air."
J.B. Priestley

„Er hat die Clownerie im Film in Gesellschaftskritik und Satire verwandelt, ohne dabei seine erstaunliche Fähigkeit einzubüßen, uns zum Lachen zu bringen ... Chaplin ist wie die meisten wahren Künstler im Grunde seines Herzens ein genialer und sanfter Anarchist, und das Lachen, das er auslöst, reinigt und versüßt nur die Luft."
J. B. Priestley

« Il a transformé le burlesque en satire et en critique sociales, sans pour autant perdre son étonnante capacité à nous faire rire... Chaplin, comme la plupart des vrais artistes, est au fond un aimable anarchiste et le rire qu'il provoque ne sert qu'à détendre et à adoucir l'atmosphère. »
J. B. Priestley

STILL FROM 'THE KID' (1921)
The child is saved. One of the cinema's most emotional moments. / Das Kind ist gerettet. Einer der bewegendsten Momente der Filmgeschichte. / L'enfant est sauvé. L'une des scènes les plus émouvantes de l'histoire du cinéma.

STILL FROM 'PAY DAY' (1922)
Exceptionally Chaplin plays a working man, but the
resulting film is hilarious. / Ausnahmsweise spielt
Chaplin einen Arbeiter. Der Film ist trotzdem
urkomisch. / Bien que Chaplin incarne pour une fois un
ouvrier, le résultat n'en est pas moins hilarant.

PORTRAIT FROM 'THE PILGRIM' (1922)
Charlie, an escaping convict, assumes the role of
pastor. / Der ausgebrochene Sträfling Charlie spielt die
Rolle des Pfarrers. / Charlot, un prisonnier en cavale, se
fait passer pour un pasteur.

UNITED ARTISTS

1923–1952

FORMATION OF UNITED ARTISTS (1919)
The biggest film stars in the world signing the
certificate of incorporation: Douglas Fairbanks, Chaplin,
Mary Pickford and director D. W. Griffith. /
Die größten Filmstars der Zeit unterzeichnen die
Gründungsurkunde ihrer neuen Firma: Douglas
Fairbanks, Chaplin, Mary Pickford und Regisseur D. W.
Griffith. / Les plus grandes stars du cinéma mondial en
train de signer l'acte de naissance de United Artists :
Douglas Fairbanks, Charlie Chaplin, Mary Pickford et le
réalisateur D. W. Griffith.

PAGE 104
STILL FROM 'THE GREAT DICTATOR' (1940)
Adenoid Hynkel, Dictator of Tomania, has dreams of
world domination. / Adenoid Hynkel, der Diktator von
Tomanien, träumt davon, die Welt zu beherrschen. /
Adenoid Hynkel, dictateur de Tomanie, rêve de devenir
le maître du monde.

ON THE SET OF 'A WOMAN OF PARIS' (1923)
Chaplin wrote and directed this sophisticated drama as
a starring vehicle for Edna Purviance. Here, the country
girl has entered the upper reaches of Parisian society
by becoming Adolphe Menjou's lover. / Chaplin schrieb
und inszenierte das anspruchsvolle Drama für Edna
Purviance. Hier ist das Mädchen vom Lande als
Adolphe Menjous Geliebte in die obersten Kreise der
Pariser Gesellschaft aufgestiegen. / Dans ce drame
sophistiqué écrit pour l'actrice Edna Purviance, une fille
de la campagne s'introduit dans la haute société
parisienne en devenant la maîtresse d'Adolphe Menjou.

STILL FROM 'A WOMAN OF PARIS' (1923)
The film has some highly erotic scenes for the period,
including a striptease during a party. / Der Film enthält
einige für die damalige Zeit sehr erotische Szenen,
darunter ein Striptease während einer Party. / Ce film
contient quelques scènes extrêmement érotiques pour
l'époque, notamment une séance de strip-tease.

"Everything I do is a dance. I think in terms of dance."
Charles Chaplin, 1968

„Alles, was ich tue, ist Tanz. Ich denke in den Begriffen des Tanzes."
Charles Chaplin, 1968

« Tout ce que je fais est une danse. Je pense en termes de danse. »
Charles Chaplin, 1968

PAGES 110/111
STILL FROM 'THE GOLD RUSH' (1925)
Location filming in arctic conditions at Truckee, California. / Außenaufnahmen unter arktischen Bedingungen bei Truckee in Kalifornien. / Tournage en extérieur dans des conditions arctiques à Truckee, en Californie.

ON THE SET OF 'A WOMAN OF PARIS' (1923)
Chaplin mimes the character's actions so that the actor can see what he wanted. / Chaplin spielt dem Schauspieler vor, was er von ihm sehen möchte. / Chaplin mime les gestes du personnage pour montrer à l'acteur ce qu'il désire.

ON THE SET OF 'THE GOLD RUSH' (1925)
Mack Swain is so hungry that he sees Charlie as a nice,
plump chicken. Here the dream is turned into reality. /
Mack Swain ist so hungrig, dass er Charlie als schönes,
fettes Brathuhn vor sich sieht. Der Traum wird hier
Wirklichkeit. / Mack Swain a tellement faim qu'il voit
Charlot comme un poulet dodu. Ici, le rêve devient
réalité.

"Without him I would never have made a film.
With Keaton he was the master of us all. His work
is always contemporary, yet eternal, and what he
brought to the cinema and to his time is
irreplaceable."
Jacques Tati

„Wenn es ihn nicht gäbe, hätte ich nie einen Film
gemacht. Zusammen mit Keaton war er unser aller
Meister. Sein Werk war stets aktuell und ist doch
zeitlos, und was er dem Kino und seiner Zeit
geschenkt hat, ist unersetzlich."
Jacques Tati

« Sans lui, je n'aurais jamais fait de films. Avec
Keaton, c'était notre maître à tous. Son œuvre est
toujours contemporaine et pourtant éternelle et ce
qu'il a apporté au cinéma et à son époque est
irremplaçable. »
Jacques Tati

STILL FROM 'THE GOLD RUSH' (1925)
The starving prospector eats a boiled boot. Chaplin
knew hunger as a child and many of his films show him
eating. / Der hungernde Goldsucher isst einen
gekochten Schuh. Chaplin wusste aus seiner Kindheit,
was Hunger bedeutet. Viele seiner Filme zeigen ihn
beim Essen. / Le chercheur d'or affamé mange une
chaussure bouillie. Chaplin a connu la faim dans son
enfance et on le voit souvent manger dans ses films.

STILL FROM 'THE GOLD RUSH' (1925)
The dance hall girl (Georgia Hale) flirts with Chaplin to
make somebody else jealous, but Chaplin takes it
seriously. / Das Mädchen aus dem Tanzsaal (Georgia
Hale) flirtet mit Chaplin, um einen anderen eifersüchtig
zu machen. Doch Charlie nimmt das Spiel ernst. / Une
entraîneuse de saloon (Georgia Hale) flirte avec Charlot
pour attiser la jalousie d'un autre, mais le malheureux se
prend au jeu.

*"He was so wonderful to work with. You didn't mind
that he told you what to do all the time, every little
thing. He was infinitely patient with actors – kind.
He knew exactly what to say and what to do to get
what he wanted."*
Georgia Hale, leading actress 'The Gold Rush'

STILL FROM 'THE GOLD RUSH' (1925)
Entangled with a dog on the dance floor. / Im Knäuel mit einem Hund am Tanzboden. / Empêtré dans la laisse d'un chien sur la piste de danse.

„Mit ihm konnte man wunderbar zusammenarbeiten. Es machte nichts, dass er einem fortwährend sagte, was man zu tun habe, jede Kleinigkeit. Er war unendlich geduldig mit den Schauspielern – nett. Er wusste genau, was er sagen und tun musste, um das zu bekommen, was er wollte."
Georgia Hale, Hauptdarstellerin, Goldrausch

« C'était merveilleux de travailler avec lui. Peu importait qu'il nous dise continuellement ce que nous avions à faire, jusqu'au moindre petit détail. Il était infiniment patient et gentil avec les acteurs. Il savait exactement quoi dire et que faire pour obtenir ce qu'il voulait. »
Georgia Hale, actrice principale de La Ruée vers l'or

ON THE SET OF 'THE GOLD RUSH' (1925)
Chaplin (centre) is tense as he directs Mack Swain. He
was totally involved with every moment that appeared
on the screen. / Angespannt gibt Chaplin (Mitte) Mack
Swain Regieanweisungen. Er steigerte sich vollkommen
in jede Leinwandszene hinein. / Chaplin (au centre)
dirige Mack Swain d'un air tendu. Il s'implique
totalement dans la moindre scène.

*"If you're smart you enter Chaplin on your books
as a son-of-a-bitch. He isn't always one, but he can
be one on occasion. I thought it better to start off
with that appellation of him in mind, then when he
behaves badly it doesn't come as quite the shock it
might otherwise be, and all his good behavior
comes as quite a pleasant surprise."*
Eddie Sutherland, assistant 'The Gold Rush'

*„Wer schlau ist, stuft Chaplin erst einmal als
Scheißkerl ein. Das ist er nicht immer, aber ab und
zu kann er einer sein. Ich dachte, es sei besser, mit
diesem Etikett im Hinterkopf bei ihm anzufangen,
dann wäre es nicht so schockierend, wenn er sich
schlecht benimmt, und all sein gutes Benehmen
wäre dann eine angenehme Überraschung."*
Eddie Sutherland, Assistent, Goldrausch

ON THE SET OF 'THE GOLD RUSH' (1925)
The director-actor reveals his irritation. Chaplin would retake and rework scenes until they flowed effortlessly into the main narrative. / Der Schauspieler und Regisseur ist gereizt. Chaplin ließ Szenen so oft wiederholen, bis sie sich nahtlos in den Handlungsverlauf einpassten. / L'acteur-réalisateur ne cache pas son irritation. Chaplin peaufine les prises jusqu'à ce qu'elles s'intègrent parfaitement dans le film.

« Ce qu'il faut, c'est noter dans ses tablettes que Chaplin est un sale type. Ce n'est pas toujours le cas, mais ça lui arrive. Je me suis dit qu'il valait mieux partir avec cette idée en tête, pour que ce ne soit pas un trop grand choc quand il se comporterait mal et pour que ses bons moments constituent une agréable surprise. »
Eddie Sutherland, assistant, La Ruée vers l'or

STILL FROM 'THE CIRCUS' (1928)
Charlie plans to steal food from a baby. / Charlie will
Essen von einem Kleinkind stehlen. / Charlot prêt à
voler la nourriture d'un bébé.

ON THE SET OF 'THE CIRCUS' (1928)
Shooting with two cameras, to provide two negatives. /
Durch das Drehen mit zwei Kameras erhielt er zwei
Negative. / Chaplin tourne avec deux caméras pour
disposer de deux négatifs.

STILL FROM 'THE CIRCUS' (1928)
With the ringmaster's ill-treated daughter (Merna Kennedy). / Mit der malträtierten Tochter (Merna Kennedy) des Zirkusdirektors. / Avec l'écuyère maltraitée (Merna Kennedy).

ON THE SET OF 'THE CIRCUS' (1928)
Chaplin effortless climbs a pole whilst escaping. / Chaplin erklimmt auf der Flucht mühelos einen Mast. / Charlot escalade agilement un poteau pour prendre la fuite.

'THE CIRCUS' (1928)
Production Sketch: Charles D. Hall captures the
dangerous nature of rope walking. / Produktionsskizze:
Charles D. Hall fängt die Gefährlichkeit des Hochseils
ein. / Croquis de Charles D. Hall illustrant le danger des
numéros de funambule.

"*[He was] a sort of Adam, from whom we are all
descended... There were two aspects of his
personality; the vagabond, but also the solitary
aristocrat, the prophet, the priest and the poet.*"
Federico Fellini

STILL FROM 'THE CIRCUS' (1928)
Monkeys upset Charlie's debut as a rope walker. /
Affen durchkreuzen Charlies ersten Auftritt als
Hochseilartist. / Des singes viennent troubler les
débuts de Charlot sur la corde raide.

„[Er war] eine Art Adam, von dem wir alle
abstammen ... Seine Persönlichkeit hatte zwei
Seiten: die des Vagabunden, aber auch die des
einsamen Aristokraten, des Propheten, des
Priesters und des Poeten."
Federico Fellini

« [Il était] une sorte d'Adam dont nous sommes tous
les descendants... Sa personnalité était double : il y
avait le vagabond, mais aussi l'aristocrate solitaire,
le prophète, le prêtre, le poète. »
Federico Fellini

ON THE SET OF 'THE CIRCUS' (1928)
Chaplin learned rope walking for the film, starting low! /
Chaplin erlernte eigens für den Film die Kunst des
Seiltanzes – und fing ganz unten an! / Pour les besoins
du film, Chaplin apprend à marcher sur une corde au ras
du sol!

ON THE SET OF 'THE CIRCUS' (1928)
Shooting the monkey-troubled tightrope sequence. /
Bei den Dreharbeiten für die Seiltanzszene mit den
störenden Affen. / Le numéro de funambule troublé par
des singes.

JOKE PHOTO (c. 1928)
Harry Crocker and Henry Bergman are in the
middle. / Harry Crocker und Henry Bergman sind in der
Mitte. / Au centre, Harry Crocker et Henry Bergman.

ON THE SET OF 'THE CIRCUS' (1928)
Still in costume, minutes after fire destroyed the set. /
Noch im Kostüm, wenige Minuten, nachdem ein Brand
das Set zerstört hat. / Encore en costume, quelques
minutes après l'incendie qui a ravagé le décor.

129

STILL FROM 'CITY LIGHTS' (1931)
The tramp saves the life of a suicidal alcoholic
millionaire (Harry Myers) and they become drinking
buddies. / Der Tramp rettet einem lebensmüden
trunksüchtigen Millionär (Harry Myers) das Leben. Die
beiden werden Saufkumpane. / Charlot sauve la vie
d'un millionnaire alcoolique et suicidaire (Harry Myers)
dont il devient un compagnon de beuverie.

STILL FROM 'CITY LIGHTS' (1931)
The tramp gets entangled in the civic statue of 'Peace
and Prosperity.' / Der Tramp verheddert sich in einer
allegorischen Statue, die „Frieden und Wohlstand"
darstellen soll. / Charlot s'empale sur la statue
symbolisant la Paix et la Prospérité.

ON THE SET OF 'CITY LIGHTS' (1931)
Chaplin mimes the scene for Virginia Cherrill, who plays
the blind flower-girl. / Chaplin spielt die Szene Virginia
Cherrill vor, die das blinde Blumenmädchen darstellt. /
Chaplin mime la scène pour Virginia Cherrill, qui joue la
fleuriste aveugle.

*"Like many self-made autocrats, Chaplin
demanded unquestioning obedience from his
associates; years of instant deference to his point
of view had persuaded him that it was the only one
that mattered."*
David Raksin

整理済み

ON THE SET OF 'CITY LIGHTS' (1931)
Filming Virginia Cherrill. / Virginia Cherrill wird
gefilmt. / En train de filmer Virginia Cherrill.

„Wie viele Autokraten von eigenen Gnaden
forderte Chaplin unbedingten Gehorsam von
seinen Mitarbeitern; dass man sich seinen
Ansichten jahrelang sofort fügte, hatte ihn zu
der Überzeugung gelangen lassen, sie seien die
einzigen, die zählten."
David Raksin

« Comme beaucoup d'autocrates ayant réussi par
leurs propres moyens, Chaplin exigeait de ses
associés une obéissance inconditionnelle. Des
années de soumission instantanée à son point de
vue l'avaient persuadé que c'était le seul valable. »
David Raksin

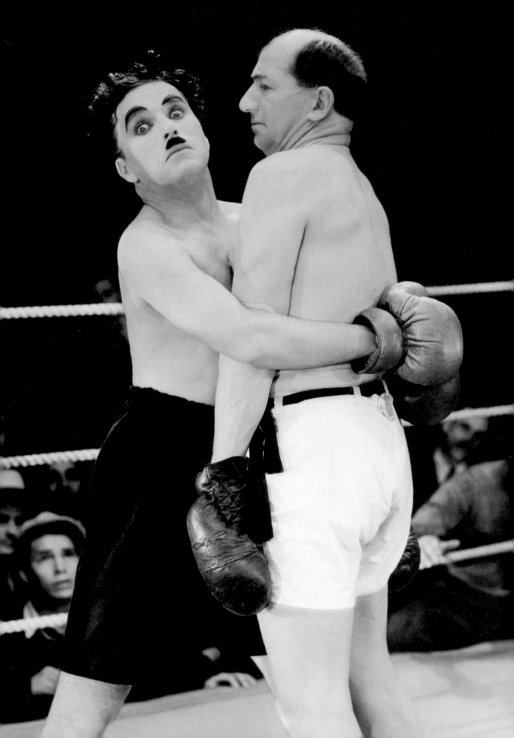

STILL FROM 'CITY LIGHTS' (1931)
Chaplin throws his head at Mann's solar plexus. The boxing sequence remained one of Chaplin's favourites. / Chaplin rammt seinen Kopf in Manns Solarplexus. Die Boxsequenz gehörte stets zu Chaplins Lieblingsszenen. / Coup de boule dans le ventre de Mann dans l'une des scènes favorites de Chaplin.

STILL FROM 'CITY LIGHTS' (1931)
The tramp needs to earn money to pay for an operation to restore the girl's sight, so he agrees to fight Hank Mann for prize money. / Da der Tramp Geld für eine Operation braucht, die dem Mädchen das Augenlicht zurückgeben kann, lässt er sich auf einen Boxkampf gegen Hank Mann ein. / Afin de pouvoir payer l'opération qui rendra la vue à la jeune fille, Charlot accepte de se battre contre Hank Mann.

'CITY LIGHTS' (1931)
Premiere: With Albert Einstein and wife. /
Uraufführung: Mit Albert Einstein und Gattin. /
Première : avec Albert Einstein et sa femme.

STILL FROM 'NICE AND FRIENDLY' (1922)
When Lord and Lady Montbatten visited from England,
Chaplin made a short unreleased home movie as a
wedding present. / Als Lord und Lady Montbatten aus
England ihn besuchten, drehte Chaplin einen kurzen
Privatfilm als Hochzeitsgeschenk. / Quand Lord et Lady
Mountbatten viennent en visite aux États-Unis, Chaplin
tourne un court métrage amateur en guise de cadeau
de mariage.

PAGES 136/137
'NEW MOVIE MAGAZINE' (NOVEMBER 1931)
Chaplin's private life fascinated the press. / Chaplins
Privatleben faszinierte die Presse. / La vie privée de
Chaplin fascine la presse.

PAGES 138/139
STILL FROM 'MODERN TIMES' (1936)
Chaplin was very concerned about the effect that
industrialisation and capitalism had on the working
people of the world, so he made a comedy infused with
his ideas. / Chaplin machte sich Sorgen über die
weltweiten Auswirkungen der Industrialisierung und der
freien Marktwirtschaft auf die Arbeiter. Deshalb drehte
er eine Komödie, in die seine Vorstellungen einflossen. /
Très préoccupé par l'effet de l'industrialisation et du
capitalisme sur les travailleurs du monde entier, Chaplin
réalise une comédie sur ce thème.

Chaplin Buries his LOVE

Past Middle Age, Possessing a Great Fortune, the Famous Comedian Says There Will Be No More Romance in His Life

By A. L. WOOLDRIDGE

Charlie Chaplin's romances have cost him great fortunes. He paid over $100,000 for his freedom from Mildred Harris. His divorce from Lita Grey ran a cost of over a million. No wonder Chaplin exclaims bitterly: "I shall never marry again."

ONE year ago, in September, Charlie Chaplin in his studio office signed his name to a check for $50,000, glanced at it briefly, then tossed it into the basket along with other letters to be mailed.

Fifty thousand dollars, the last of a $625,000 cash alimony payment to Lita Grey! There remained two more years during which he must place to her credit $1,000 a month. Next year he will establish a trust fund of $200,000 for the two sons Lita bore him and the slate will be clean. Eight hundred and fifty thousand dollars for a wife of less than two years; more than a million, counting costs, for a mistake he will remember the rest of his life.

"I shall never marry again," he said to me one day when the settlement with Lita had been adjusted. "This is the finish."

It wasn't the loss of the million which hurt. He had other millions at his command. It was the feeling that he was alone in the world, rich, yet unloved by any wholesome, honest young woman to whom he could turn with pride. His marriages to Mildred Harris and Lita Grey had left him miserable—hating the

fate and circumstances which brought them together. "I shall never marry again!" he said.

I believe he meant it. I believe he means it still. The story coming recently from France that he was enamoured of Mizzi Muller, a Czecho-Slovakian girl, was totally unwarranted. She was his secretary-interpreter, nothing more.

TWICE—and only twice, I happen to know—has Charlie been really in love. One occasion is only a memory, yet it is to that memory he oftenest turns now in hours of retrospection. He never has and never will forget little Hetty Kelly, the girl he knew in London streets during the days when both were poor. Whenever he goes to London, he still takes time to

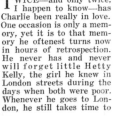

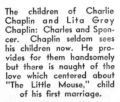

The children of Charlie Chaplin and Lita Grey Chaplin: Charles and Spencer. Chaplin seldom sees his children now. He provides for them handsomely but there is naught of the love which centered about "The Little Mouse," child of his first marriage.

Pacific and Atlantic Photos

THREE WOMEN WHO PLAYED A VITAL PART IN CHAPLIN'S LIFE

visit the places where he and Hetty, hardly more than children, dreamed their dreams of love and envisioned the time when they could earn enough to be married. No woman ever has displaced the image of her which Chaplin still holds in his heart. No one ever will. Yet he never mentions her name. Once in his book, "My Trip Abroad," written in 1922, he told the story of Hetty—told it frankly, honestly, then closed the chapter forever, so far as its recital to the outside world is concerned.

"The taxi is going up Kennington Road, along Kennington Park," he wrote. "Kennington Park! How depressing Kennington Park is. How depressing to me are all parks. The loneliness of them. One never goes to a park unless one is lonesome. And lonesomeness is sad. The symbol of sadness, that's a park.

"But I am fascinated with it now. I am lonesome and want to be. I want to commune with myself and the years that are gone. The years that were passed in the shadow of this same Kennington Park. I want to sit on its benches again in spite of their treacherous bleakness, in spite of the drabness.

"Kennington Gate. That has its memories. Sad, sweet, rapidly recurring memories. 'Twas here, my first appointment with Hetty. How I was dolled up in my little tight-fitting frock coat, hat and cane! I was quite the dude as I watched every street car until four o'clock, waiting for Hetty to step off, smiling as she saw me waiting.

"I get out and stand there for a few moments at Kennington Gate. . . .

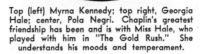

Top (left) Myrna Kennedy; top right, Georgia Hale; center, Pola Negri. Chaplin's greatest friendship has been and is with Miss Hale, who played with him in "The Gold Rush." She understands his moods and temperament.

I am seeing a lad of nineteen, dressed in the pink, with fluttering heart, waiting, waiting for the moment of the day when he and happiness walked along the road.

"The road is so alluring now. It beckons for another walk, and as I hear a street car approaching I turn eagerly, for the moment almost expecting to see the same trim Hetty step off, smiling.

"The car stops. A couple of men get off. An old woman. Some children. But no Hetty.

"Hetty is gone. So is the lad with the tight-fitting frock coat and the little cane."

THERE Charlie lets the story of Hetty end. The ensuing tragedy, he omits. What he might have added was that when he came to America in 1909 to appear in the burlesque skit, "A Night in a London Music Hall," Hetty was dancing in the chorus of a revue. When he prepared to board the boat, she tearfully placed her arms about his neck and bade him goodbye and godspeed and they again plighted their troth, as both of their hearts ached.

"I'll be back for you!" Charlie said.

Thereafter Hetty's sister, Edith, married Frank Gould, the son of the American multi-millionaire, Jay Gould, and Hetty soon was clothed in silks and her fingers bejeweled. When Charlie's New York engagement ended two years later he hurried back to London, his purse containing more than it ever had held in all his life. He was going right back to his Hetty, the girl in little cheap dresses, unsophisticated, unspoiled, and still obscure.

"My Hetty!" he said in his eagerness.

Alas for his illusions! Time and circumstance had made a change just as time and circumstance always make a change. The little dancing chorus girl in her almost shabby dresses had been transformed into a (Please turn to page 82)

"The Little Mouse," tragic child of Chaplin's union with Mildred Harris, lies buried in Inglewood Cemetery. The little grave is by the side of a pool shaded by the boughs of pepper trees.

'MODERN TIMES' (1936)
Production Sketch / Produktionsskizze / Croquis des décors

'MODERN TIMES' (1936)
Chaplin at factory location used in the film. / Chaplin vor der Fabrik, die im Film verwendet wurde. / Chaplin devant l'usine qui sert de décor au film.

ON THE SET OF 'MODERN TIMES' (1936)
Adjusting Paulette Goddard's costume and make-up. /
Beim Richten von Paulette Goddards Kostüm und
Maske. / En train de retoucher le costume et le
maquillage de Paulette Goddard.

STILL FROM 'MODERN TIMES' (1936)
An involuntary morning dip. / Ein unfreiwilliges
Morgenbad. / Un plongeon matinal bien involontaire.

STILL FROM 'MODERN TIMES' (1936)
The worker driven crazy by the incessant production
line. / Der Arbeiter wird vom unaufhörlich laufenden
Fließband zum Wahnsinn getrieben. / L'ouvrier rendu
fou par le travail à la chaîne.

*"I am not a Communist. I am a human being, and I
think I know the reactions of human beings. The
Communists are no different from anyone else;
whether they lose an arm or a leg, they suffer as all
of us do, and die as all of us die. And the
Communist mother is the same as any other
mother. When she receives the tragic news that her
sons will not return, she weeps as other mothers
weep. I do not have to be a Communist to know
that. And at this moment Russian mothers are
doing a lot of weeping and their sons a lot of
dying..."*
Charles Chaplin, San Francisco, May 1942

STILL FROM 'MODERN TIMES' (1936)
Charlie inadvertently becomes leader of Communist demonstration. / Charlie wird unfreiwillig zum Anführer der kommunistischen Demonstration. / Charlot se retrouve involontairement la tête d'une manifestation communiste.

„Ich bin kein Kommunist. Ich bin ein Mensch, und ich denke, ich weiß, wie Menschen reagieren. Die Kommunisten unterscheiden sich nicht von allen anderen: Ob sie einen Arm oder ein Bein verlieren, sie leiden wie wir alle, und sie sterben, wie wir alle sterben. Und die kommunistische Mutter ist genau wie jede andere Mutter. Wenn sie die tragische Nachricht erhält, dass ihr Sohn nicht zurückkehrt, weint sie, wie andere Mütter weinen. Ich muss kein Kommunist sein, um das zu wissen. Und in diesem Augenblick gibt es unter russischen Müttern ein großes Weinen und unter ihren Söhnen ein großes Sterben ..."
Charles Chaplin, San Francisco, Mai 1942

« Je ne suis pas communiste. Je suis un être humain et je pense connaître les réactions des humains. Les communistes ne sont pas différents des autres; s'ils perdent un bras ou une jambe, ils souffrent comme tout le monde et meurent comme chacun d'entre nous. Et la mère communiste est semblable à toute autre mère. Quand elle reçoit la tragique nouvelle que son fils ne reviendra pas, elle pleure comme pleurent toutes les mères. Je n'ai pas besoin d'être communiste pour le savoir. Et à l'heure actuelle, les mères russes pleurent beaucoup et leurs fils meurent beaucoup... »
Charles Chaplin, San Francisco, mai 1942

STILL FROM 'THE GREAT DICTATOR' (1940)
Chaplin plays a Jewish barber who is a hero during
World War One before losing his memory. / Chaplin
spielt einen jüdischen Barbier, der im Ersten Weltkrieg
zum Helden wird und dann sein Gedächtnis verliert. /
Chaplin incarne un barbier juif qui fut un héros de la
Première Guerre mondiale avant de perdre la mémoire.

**ON THE SET OF 'THE GREAT DICTATOR'
(1940)**
Chaplin, in costume as dictator Adenoid Hynkel,
inspects the camera set-up. / Chaplin prüft im Kostüm
des Diktators Adenoid Hynkel die Aufstellung der
Kamera. / Chaplin, dans le costume du dictateur
Adenoid Hynkel, inspecte la caméra.

PAGES 148/149
**ON THE SET OF 'THE GREAT DICTATOR'
(1940)**
Filming the rally sequence. Although 'Modern Times'
was Chaplin's first sound picture, he only sang a
nonsense song in it. For this film he spoke on film for
the first time. / Bei den Dreharbeiten zur
Kundgebungssequenz. *Moderne Zeiten* war Chaplins
erster Tonfilm, er sang aber nur ein Nonsenslied. Für
Der große Diktator sprach er das erste Mal vor der
Kamera. / La scène du meeting. Bien que *Les Temps
modernes* soit le premier film sonore de Chaplin,
il se contente d'y chanter une chanson. C'est dans
Le Dictateur qu'on l'entend parler pour la première fois.

STILL FROM 'THE GREAT DICTATOR' (1940)
Too late! The stormtroopers find them! / Zu spät! Die
Sturmtruppen finden sie! / Trop tard! Les sections
d'assaut les retrouvent!

STILL FROM 'THE GREAT DICTATOR' (1940)
The Jewish barber is unaware that fascists are
persecuting the Jews. Paulette Goddard warns him to
keep quiet. / Dem jüdischen Barbier ist nicht klar, dass
die Faschisten Juden verfolgen. Paulette Goddard
ermahnt ihn, still zu sein. / Le barbier juif ignore tout
des persécutions que les fascistes font subir à son
peuple. Paulette Goddard le met en garde.

STILL FROM 'THE GREAT DICTATOR' (1940)
Adenoid Hynkel resorts to less than diplomatic means
with visiting dictator Benzino Napaloni (Jack Oakie). /
Adenoid Hynkel verhält sich recht undiplomatisch
gegenüber seinem Kollegen auf Staatsbesuch, Benzini
Napaloni (Jack Oakie). / Adenoid Hynkel frôle l'incident
diplomatique avec le dictateur Benzini Napaloni (Jack
Oakie).

"Charles Chaplin is the only artist who holds the
secret weapon of mortal laughter. Not the laugh of
superficial gibing that self-complacently
underrates the enemy and ignores the danger, but
rather the profound laughter of the sage who
despises physical violence, even the threat of
death, because behind it he has discovered the
spiritual weakness, stupidity, and falseness of his
antagonist."
Rudolph Arnheim on 'The Great Dictator'

STILL FROM 'THE GREAT DICTATOR' (1940)
The dictator burns up the dance floor with the goose
step. / Der Tanzboden qualmt unter dem Stechschritt
des Diktators. / Le pas de l'oie sur la piste de danse.

„Charles Chaplin ist der einzige Künstler, der über
die Geheimwaffe des tödlichen Gelächters ver-
fügt – nicht das Lachen des oberflächlichen Spotts,
der den Feind selbstgefällig unterschätzt und die
Gefahr ignoriert, sondern das tiefgründige
Gelächter des Weisen, der körperliche Gewalt,
sogar die Todesdrohung verabscheut, weil er
hinter ihr die geistige Schwäche, Dummheit und
Falschheit seines Gegenspielers entdeckt hat."
Rudolph Arnheim über Der große Diktator

« Charles Chaplin est le seul artiste qui détient
l'arme secrète du rire mortel. Non pas le rire
superficiel du railleur suffisant qui sous-estime
l'ennemi et ignore le danger, mais le rire profond
du sage qui méprise la violence physique et même
la menace de la mort, car derrière, il a découvert la
faiblesse spirituelle, la stupidité et la fausseté de
son adversaire. »
Rudolph Arnheim à propos du Dictateur

STILL FROM 'THE GREAT DICTATOR' (1940)
Chaplin makes two speeches in the film, one as the
dictator saying that he will squash the Jews, and the
other as the barber saying that we must love and
tolerate each other. Interestingly, the rhythm and
passion of both speeches are very similar. / Chaplin hält
in dem Film zwei Reden: In der ersten gibt er als
Diktator bekannt, dass er die Juden ausrotten wird, in
der anderen ruft er als Barbier zu Toleranz und
Nächstenliebe auf. Interessanterweise ähneln sich
beide Reden in Rhythmus und Leidenschaft. / Chaplin
prononce deux discours rythmés et déclamés de façon
assez similaire, l'un dans le rôle du dictateur déclarant
qu'il va écraser les juifs, l'autre dans le rôle du barbier
prônant l'amour et la tolérance.

STILL FROM 'MONSIEUR VERDOUX' (1947)
Monsieur Verdoux believes that he has taken the
poison intended for Annabella Bonheur. / Monsieur
Verdoux glaubt, er habe das Gift geschluckt, das für
Annabella Bonheur bestimmt war. / Monsieur Verdoux
(Chaplin) croit avoir ingéré le poison destiné à
Annabella Bonheur (Martha Raye).

PAGES 158/159
ON THE SET OF 'MONSIEUR VERDOUX' (1947)
Verdoux had killed a number of wives for their money,
but every attempt on Annabella ends in disaster. /
Verdoux hatte mehrere Ehefrauen wegen ihres
Vermögens erfolgreich ins Jenseits befördert, doch
sämtliche Mordversuche an Annabella enden in einer

Katastrophe. / Verdoux est parvenu à assassiner
plusieurs de ses épouses pour hériter de leur fortune,
mais toutes les tentatives de meurtre d'Annabella
tournent au fiasco.

ON THE SET OF 'MONSIEUR VERDOUX' (1947)
French director Robert Florey (right) was happy to
supply technical information about the French settings
of the film. / Der französische Regisseur Robert Florey
(rechts) steuerte gerne technische Informationen zu
den französischen Handlungsorten bei. / Le réalisateur
français Robert Florey (à droite) aide Chaplin à créer un
décor représentant la France.

"One murder makes a villain... millions a hero.
Numbers sanctify, my good friend."
Monsieur Verdoux, 'Monsieur Verdoux' (1947)

„Ein Mord macht einen Bösewicht ... Millionen Morde
einen Helden. Zahlen heiligen, mein guter Freund."
Monsieur Verdoux, *Monsieur Verdoux* (1947)

« Un meurtre fait de vous un bandit, des millions,
un héros. Le nombre sanctifie ! »
Monsieur Verdoux, *Monsieur Verdoux* (1947)

STILL FROM 'MONSIEUR VERDOUX' (1947)
Verdoux goes to the guillotine. / Verdoux schreitet zur
Guillotine. / Verdoux en route pour la guillotine.

ON THE SET OF 'MONSIEUR VERDOUX' (1947)
In his final speech Chaplin says that as a mass murderer
he is an amateur in comparision to the political world. /
In seiner Abschlussrede meint Verdoux, als
Massenmörder sei er nur ein kleiner Fisch im Vergleich
zur Politik. / Dans son discours final, Chaplin déclare
qu'un tueur en série n'est qu'un amateur par rapport
aux chefs d'État.

STILL FROM 'LIMELIGHT' (1952)
Age makes way for youth... Comedian Calvero (Chaplin) is forlorn after 'dying' on the stage as dancer Thereza (Claire Bloom) regains the use of her legs. / Das Alter macht der Jugend Platz: Nach seinem Bühnentod ist der Clown Calvero (Chaplin) verzweifelt, als die Tänzerin Thereza (Claire Bloom) ihre Beine wieder gebrauchen kann. / La vieillesse cède la place à la jeunesse... Le comédien Calvero (Chaplin) « meurt » sur scène, tandis que la danseuse Thereza (Claire Bloom) retrouve l'usage de ses jambes.

STILL FROM 'LIMELIGHT' (1952)
Thereza has stage fright before her big performance, so
Calvero slaps her onto the stage. They are dependent
upon each other. / Thereza hat vor ihrem großen
Auftritt Lampenfieber, so dass Calvero sich gezwungen
sieht, sie mit Ohrfeigen auf die Bühne zu treiben. Sie
sind voneinander abhängig. / Pour aider Thereza à
surmonter son trac, Calvero l'envoie de force sur scène.
Chacun a besoin de l'autre.

PAGES 164/165
ON THE SET OF 'LIMELIGHT' (1952)
Chaplin (center, white hair), plans the opening scene of
the ballet, with assistant director Robert Aldrich behind
him in glasses. / Chaplin (Mitte, weißes Haar) plant die
Eröffnungsszene des Balletts; hinter ihm steht
Regieassistent Robert Aldrich (mit Brille). / Chaplin
(au centre, avec les cheveux blancs) prépare la scène
d'ouverture du ballet avec son assistant Robert Aldrich
(l'homme aux lunettes).

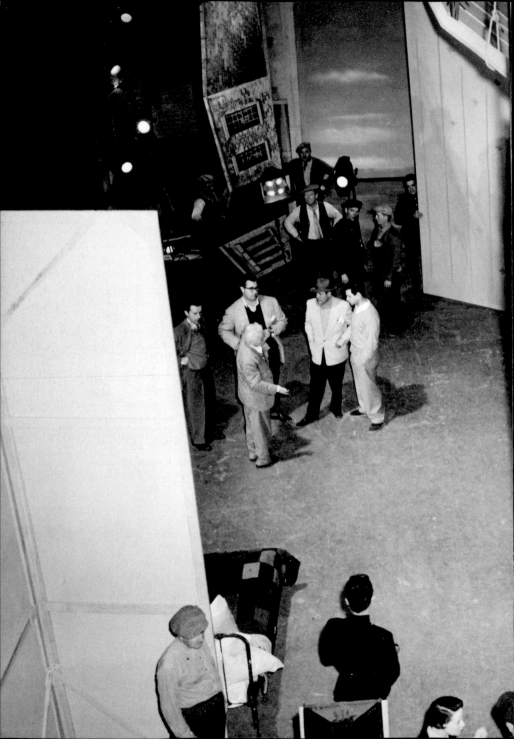

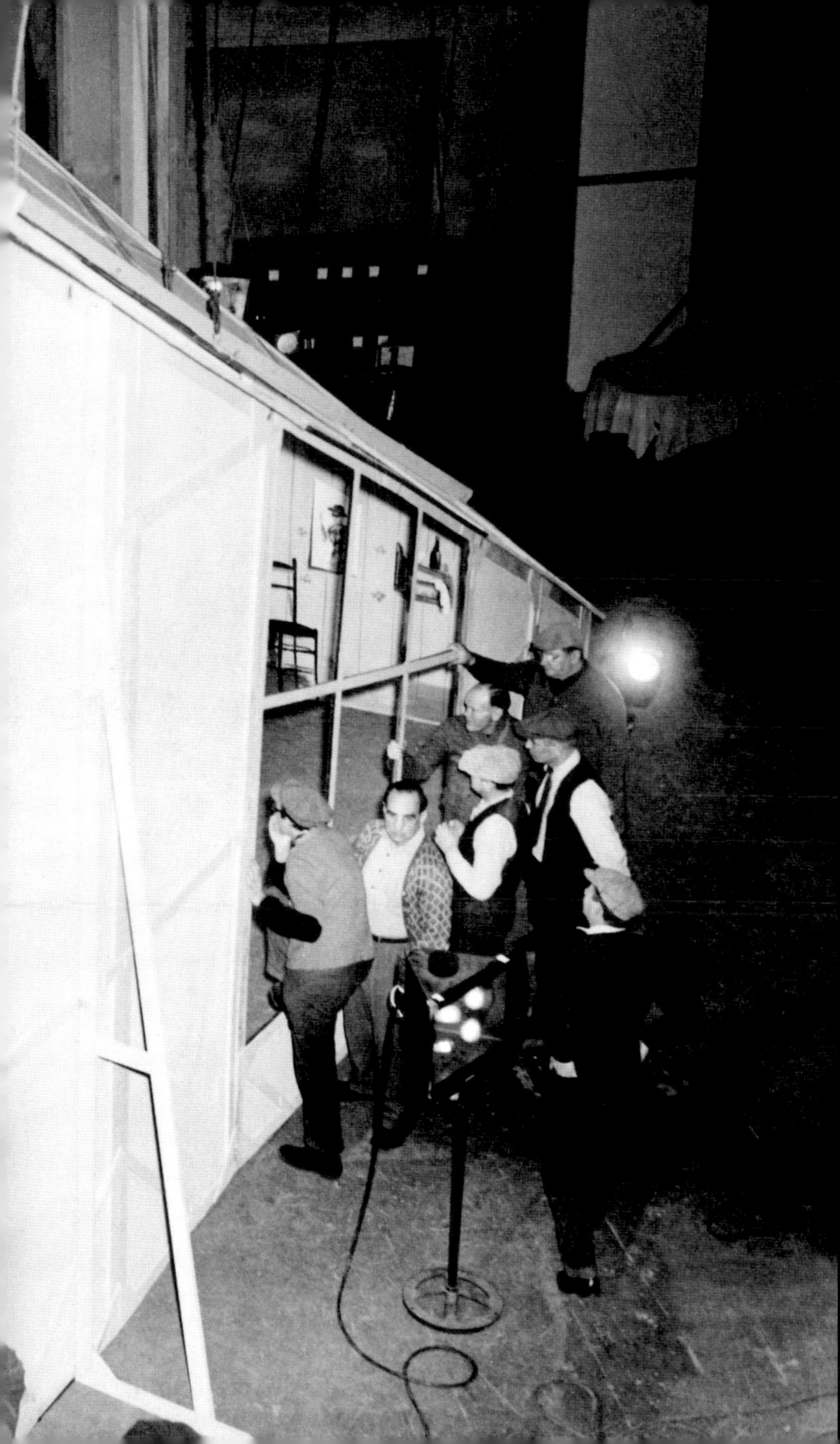

STILL FROM 'LIMELIGHT' (1952)
Chaplin as the clown in the ballet, with his son Charles
Jr. as the policeman, and his brother Wheeler Dryden
as the other clown. / Chaplin als Clown im Ballett. Sein
Sohn Charles jr. spielt den Polizisten und sein Bruder
Wheeler Dryden einen weiteren Clown. / Chaplin en
clown de ballet, avec son fils Charles Jr. dans le rôle du
policier et son frère Wheeler Dryden dans celui de
l'autre clown.

*"We can never admire enough his grasp of detail,
the clockwork precision which each of his films
represents, and which is perhaps the essence of his
genius – an element even more important than his
art of the gag."*
Buster Keaton, 1952

STILL FROM 'LIMELIGHT' (1952)
For his final performance, assisted by Buster Keaton, Calvero is a hit with the crowd. / Calvaros letzter Auftritt wird mit der Unterstützung von Buster Keaton zu einem großen Publikumserfolg. / Pour son dernier spectacle, Calvero fait un tabac avec l'aide de Buster Keaton.

„Wir können sein Verständnis für das Detail nie genug bewundern, die uhrwerkgleiche Präzision, die jeder seiner Filme verkörpert und die vielleicht das Wesen seines Genies ausmacht – ein Element, das vielleicht wichtiger ist als seine Gagkunst."
Buster Keaton, 1952

« Nous n'admirerons jamais assez sa maîtrise du détail, la précision d'horloger que représente chacun de ses films et qui constitue peut-être l'essence même de son génie, un élément encore plus important que son sens du gag. »
Buster Keaton, 1952

BRITISH PRODUCTIONS
1957–1967

STILL FROM 'A KING IN NEW YORK' (1957)
From the moment he arrives in New York, King Shahdov
is beset with reporters all wanting a juicy story. TV
reporter Ann Kay's (Dawn Addams) approach is none
too subtle. / Von dem Augenblick an, in dem er in New
York ankommt, wird König Shahdov von
schlagzeilenhungrigen Reportern belagert. Auch
Fernsehreporterin Ann Kay (Dawn Addams) geht nicht
besonders subtil vor. / Dès son arrivée à New York, le
roi Shahdov est assailli de journalistes à l'affût de
nouvelles croustillantes. La journaliste de télévision
Ann Kay (Dawn Addams) n'y va pas par quatre chemins.

PAGE 168
ON THE SET OF 'A KING IN NEW YORK' (1957)
Chaplin, aged 68, plays a deposed monarch who is
trying to get his utopian ideas about atomic energy off
the ground. / Chaplin spielt im Alter von 68 Jahren
einen abgesetzten Monarchen, der versucht, für seine
utopischen Vorstellungen über Kernenergie Abnehmer
zu finden. / Chaplin, âgé de 68 ans, interprète un
monarque détrôné qui tente d'imposer ses idées
utopiques concernant l'énergie nucléaire.

ON THE SET OF 'A KING IN NEW YORK' (1957)
Chaplin shows Dawn Addams how to wash her leg. /
Chaplin zeigt Dawn Addams, wie sie ihr Bein waschen
soll. / Chaplin montre à Dawn Addams comment se
savonner la jambe.

STILL FROM 'A KING IN NEW YORK' (1957)
Shahdov transforms the objects on the dinner table to demonstrate how dentists are always on the phone. / Shahdov zweckentfremdet die Gegenstände auf dem Esstisch, um zu demonstrieren, wie sich Zahnärzte am Telefon verhalten. / Shahdov imitant les dentistes toujours pendus au téléphone.

ON THE SET OF 'A COUNTESS FROM HONG KONG' (1967)
Chaplin attacks his 77th birthday cake, with Oona Chaplin, Melanie Griffith and Sophia Loren behind him. / Chaplin schneidet an seinem 77. Geburtstag die Torte an. Hinter ihm stehen Oona Chaplin, Melanie Griffith und Sophia Loren. / Chaplin attaque le gâteau de son 77ᵉ anniversaire en compagnie d'Oona Chaplin, de Melanie Griffith et de Sophia Loren.

ON THE SET OF 'A COUNTESS FROM HONG KONG' (1967)

Although Marlon Brando was a huge fan of Chaplin, their differing methods of working caused friction. / Obwohl Marlon Brando ein großer Verehrer Chaplins war, führten ihre unterschiedlichen Arbeitsweisen zu Reibungen. / Malgré l'immense admiration de Marlon Brando pour Chaplin, les divergences entre leurs méthodes de travaillent provoquent des frictions.

"I like making pictures, and I like acting in them, and I suppose that I shall always be a bit of film."
Charles Chaplin, 'Adelphi Magazine' (January 1925)

„Ich mache gerne Filme, und ich spiele gerne in ihnen, und vermutlich werde ich stets ein Stück Film sein."
Charles Chaplin, *Adelphi Magazine* (Januar 1925)

« J'aime faire des films et j'aime jouer dedans et je suppose que je laisserai toujours un peu de moi sur la pellicule. »
Charles Chaplin, *Adelphi Magazine* (janvier 1925)

ON THE SET OF 'A COUNTESS FROM HONG KONG' (1967)

Marlon Brando plays an American millionaire who falls in love with beautiful Russian stowaway Sophia Loren. / Marlon Brando spielt einen amerikanischen Millionär. Er verliebt sich in Sophia Loren, die eine hübsche blinde Passagierin aus Russland darstellt. / Marlon Brando incarne un millionnaire américain qui s'éprend d'une belle passagère clandestine russe, Sophia Loren.

PAGES 176/177
LONDON (1959)

Chaplin visited the London of his childhood to help trigger memories for his autobiography. / Chaplin besuchte das London seiner Kindheit, um Erinnerungen für seine Autobiografie wachzurufen. / Chaplin visite le Londres de son enfance pour raviver ses souvenirs en vue de son autobiographie.

3
CHRONOLOGY

CHRONOLOGIE
CHRONOLOGY

CENTRAL LONDON POOR LAW SCHOOL (1897)
Chaplin (circled, center left), aged 7. / Chaplin (Mitte links) im Alter von sieben Jahren. / Chaplin (cerclé à gauche du centre) à l'école de Hanwell, à l'âge de 7 ans.

PAGE 178
ON THE SET OF 'LIMELIGHT' (1952)

1889 16 April: Birth of Charles Chaplin.

1892 Separation of Chaplin's parents.

1896–1898 Chaplin inmate in Hanwell School for destitute children.

1898–1902 First professional job, with *Eight Lancashire Lads* music hall act.

1901 9 May: Death of Chaplin's father aged 37.

1903–1906 Tours as Billy in play, *Sherlock Holmes*.

1905 October–November: Appears at Duke of York's Theatre, London as Billy, in *The Painful Predicament of Sherlock Holmes* and *Sherlock Holmes*.

1906 March: Returns to music hall stage in sketch *Repairs*.

1907 May–July: Tours with music hall act *Caseys Court Circus*.

1908 21 February: Signs first contract with Fred Karno; plays in Karno sketches *The Football Match, Skating, Mumming Birds, Jimmy the Fearless*.

1910–1912 Tours United States with Karno sketch company.

1912 October: Embarks on second Karno tour of United States.

1913 5 September: Signs contract with Keystone Film Company. 29 November: Final appearance on stage with Karno company.

1914 2 February: Release of first film, *Making a Living*. 7 February: Release of *Kid Auto Races*, the first film in which Chaplin wore the famous tramp costume. February–December: Appears in 35 films for Keystone film company. 14 December: Release of *Tillie's Punctured Romance*, first feature-length slapstick comedy.

1915 Directs and stars in 14 two-reel films for Essanay Film Manufacturing Company.

1916–1917 Produces, directs and stars in 12 two-reel films for distribution by the Mutual Film Corporation.

1918 January: Opens own studio. 23 October: Marries Mildred Harris.

1918–1922 Produces, directs and stars in 8 films for release by First National Exhibitors' Circuit.

1919 5 February: United Artists officially created.

1920 30 November: Mildred Harris granted divorce.

1921 6 February: Release of *The Kid*, Chaplin's first feature-length film. 3 September–12 October: Triumphal return to Europe.

1923 28 January: Chaplin and Pola Negri announce their engagement. 1 March: It is broken off. 2 March: It is back on. 28 June: It is definitely off. 6 September: Release of Chaplin's first UA film, *A Woman of Paris*.

1924 26 November: Marries Lita Grey, by whom has two children, Charles Spencer (1925–1968) and Sydney Earl (born 1926).

1927 12 August: Lita Grey granted divorce.

1931 Chaplin's first film using sound, *City Lights*.

1931–1932 Extended world tour.

1932 July: Begins liaison with Paulette Goddard.

1936 17 February–3 June: Following release of *Modern Times*, extended world tour with Paulette Goddard.

1940 15 October: Premiere of Chaplin's first talking picture, *The Great Dictator*.

1942 4 June: Paulette Goddard granted divorce from marriage alleged to have taken place in Far East in 1936.

1943 16 June: Chaplin marries Oona O'Neill.

1944 10 February–14 April: Chaplin on trial for various alleged offences relating to liaison with actress Joan Barry. 13 December–2 January: Paternity suit against Chaplin. Jury fails to agree.

1945 4–17 April: Second paternity suit brought on behalf of Joan Barry. Majority jury finds against Chaplin.

1952 17 September: Chaplin and family set sail for London for premiere of *Limelight*. 19 September: Chaplin's permit for re-entry to United States rescinded.

1953 Chaplins take up permanent residence in Manoir de Ban, Corsier-sur-Vevey, Switzerland.

1957 12 September: London premiere of Chaplin's first film made outside Hollywood, *A King in New York*.

1964 Publication of *My Autobiography*.

1967 January: Release of Chaplin's last film *A Countess from Hong Kong*. Chaplin continues to work until death, composing new music for his silent films, and preparing a never-to-be-made script, *The Freak*.

1972 16 April: Received honorary Academy Award in Hollywood.

1975 4 March: Knighted by H.M. Queen Elizabeth II.

1977 25 December: Chaplin dies in his sleep at his home.

1978 1 March: Theft of Chaplin's body from his grave. It was recovered on 17 March and Gantcho Ganev and Roman Wardas were convicted.

1991 27 September: Death of Oona Chaplin.

CHRONOLOGIE

1889 16. April: Charles Chaplin wird geboren.

1892 Chaplins Eltern trennen sich.

1896–1898 Chaplin wird in die Hanwell-Schule für bedürftige Kinder eingewiesen.

1898–1902 Erste bezahlte Arbeit in der Varieténummer „Eight Lancashire Lads" („Die acht Burschen aus Lancashire").

1901 9. Mai: Chaplins Vater stirbt im Alter von 37 Jahren.

1903–1906 Geht als Billy in dem Stück *Sherlock Holmes* auf Tournee.·

1905 Oktober–November: Tritt als Billy am Londoner Duke of York's Theatre in *The Painful Predicament of Sherlock Holmes* und *Sherlock Holmes* auf.

1906 März: Rückkehr auf die Varitébühne mit dem Sketch *Repairs*.

1907 Mai–Juli: Geht mit der Varieténummer *Caseys Court Circus* auf Tournee.

1908 21. Februar: Schließt seinen ersten Vertrag mit Fred Karno und tritt in den Karno-Sketchen *The Football Match, Skating, Mumming Birds* und *Jimmy the Fearless* auf.

1910–1912 Geht mit Karnos Sketchtruppe auf Tournee durch die USA.

1912 Oktober: Geht zum zweiten Mal mit der Karno-Truppe auf Tournee durch die USA.

1913 5. September: Schließt einen Vertrag mit der Keystone Film Company. 29. November: Letzter Bühnenauftritt mit der Karno-Truppe.

1914 2. Februar: Premiere seines ersten Films *Making a Living (Man schlägt sich durch)*. 7. Februar: Premiere des Films *Kid Auto Races*, in dem Chaplin erstmals das berühmte Tramp-Kostüm trägt. Februar–Dezember: Tritt in 35 Keystone-Filmen auf. 14. Dezember: Premiere von *Tillie's Punctured Romance*, der ersten abendfüllenden Slapstick-Komödie.

1915 Übernimmt Regie und Hauptrolle in 14 Zweiaktern für die Essanay Film Manufacturing Company.

1916–1917 Übernimmt Produktion, Regie und Hauptrolle in zwölf Zweiaktern im Verleih der Mutual Film Corporation.

1918 Januar: Eröffnet sein eigenes Studio. 23. Oktober: Heirat mit Mildred Harris.

1918–1922 Übernimmt Produktion, Regie und Hauptrolle in acht Filmen, die über den First National Exhibitors' Circuit in den Verleih kommen.

1919 5. Februar: Offizielle Gründung von United Artists (UA).

1920 30. November: Mildred Harris reicht die Scheidung ein.

1921 6. Februar: Premiere von *The Kid (Der Vagabund und das Kind)*, Chaplins erstem abendfüllendem Spielfilm. 3. September–12. Oktober: Triumphale Rückkehr nach Europa.

1923 28. Januar: Chaplin und Pola Negri geben ihre Verlobung bekannt. 11. März: Die Verlobung wird abgesagt. 2. März: Die Verlobung wird erneuert. 28. Juni: Die Verlobung wird endgültig abgesagt. 6. September: Premiere von *A Woman of Paris (Die Nächte einer schönen Frau/Eine Frau in Paris)*, Chaplins erstem UA-Film.

1924 26. November: Heirat mit Lita Grey, mit der er zwei Kinder hat: Charles Spencer (1925–1968) und Sydney Earl (*1926).

1927 12. August: Lita Grey reicht die Scheidung ein.

1931 Bei *City Lights (Lichter der Großstadt)* verwendet Chaplin erstmals Tonaufnahmen.

1931–1932 Ausgiebige Welttournee.

1932 Juli: Beginn der Beziehung zu Paulette Goddard.

1936 17. Februar–3. Juni: Nach der Premiere von *Modern Times (Moderne Zeiten)* geht er mit Paulette Goddard auf große Welttournee.

1940 15. Oktober: Premiere von *The Great Dictator (Der große Diktator)*, Chaplins erstem Tonfilm.

1942 4. Juni: Paulette Goddard reicht die Scheidung einer Ehe ein, die angeblich 1936 in Fernost geschlossen wurde.

1943 16. Juni: Heirat mit Oona O'Neill.

1944 10. Februar–14. April: Im Zusammenhang mit einer Beziehung zur Schauspielerin Joan Barry wird Chaplin wegen zahlreicher angeblicher Vergehen

vor Gericht gestellt. 13. Dezember–2. Januar: Vaterschaftsklage gegen Chaplin. Die Geschworenen können sich nicht einigen.

1945 4.–17. April: Zweite Vaterschaftsklage durch Joan Barry. Die Mehrheit der Geschworenen entscheidet sich gegen Chaplin.

1952 17. September: Für die Premiere von *Limelight* (*Rampenlicht*) reist Chaplin mit seiner Familie per Schiff nach London. 19. September: Chaplin wird die Wiedereinreise in die Vereinigten Staaten verweigert.

1953 Chaplin lässt sich dauerhaft im Manoir de Ban in Corsier-sur-Vevey in der Schweiz nieder.

1957 12. September: Londoner Premiere von *A King in New York* (*Ein König in New York*), Chaplins erstem Film, der nicht in Hollywood entstanden ist.

1964 Veröffentlichung von *My Autobiography* (*Die Geschichte meines Lebens*).

1967 Januar: Premiere seines letzten Films *A Countess from Hong Kong* (*Die Gräfin von Hongkong*). Chaplin arbeitet bis zu seinem Tod weiter, komponiert neue Musiken für seine Stummfilme und bereitet ein Drehbuch mit dem Titel *The Freak* vor, das nie verfilmt wird.

'REPAIRS' (1906)
Charles Chaplin (center) with Sydney as the painter on the ladder. / Charles Chaplin (Mitte) und sein Bruder Sydney (als Maler auf der Leiter). / Charles Chaplin (au centre) et son frère Sydney (le peintre sur l'échelle).

1972 16. April: Erhält in Hollywood einen Ehren-Oscar.

1975 4. März: Wird von Königin Elisabeth II. zum Ritter geschlagen.

1977 25. Dezember: Chaplin stirbt zu Hause im Schlaf.

1978 1. März: Chaplins Leichnam wird aus dem Grab gestohlen. Nach dem Wiederauffinden am 17. März werden Gantcho Ganev und Roman Wardas wegen Störung der Totenruhe verurteilt.

1991 27. September: Tod von Oona Chaplin.

CHRONOLOGIE

1889 16 avril : naissance de Charles Chaplin.

1892 Séparation des parents de Charles.

1896–1898 Charles est placé en pensionnat dans une école pour enfants déshérités.

1898–1902 Il décroche son premier emploi dans la troupe de music-hall des *Eight Lancashire Lads*.

1901 9 mai : décès de son père à l'âge de 37 ans.

1903–1906 Part en tournée en interprétant le rôle de Billy dans une pièce intitulée *Sherlock Holmes*.

1905 Octobre–novembre : joue le rôle de Billy dans *The Painful Predicament of Sherlock Holmes* et *Sherlock Holmes* au Duke of York's Theatre de Londres.

1906 Mars : revient au music-hall dans le sketch *Repairs*.

1907 Mai-juillet : part en tournée pour la revue de music-hall *Casey's Court Circus*.

1908 21 février : signe son premier contrat avec Fred Karno et se produit dans les sketches *The Football Match*, *Skating*, *Mumming Birds* et *Jimmy the Fearless*.

1910–1912 Par en tournée aux États-Unis avec la troupe de Karno.

1912 Octobre : entame une deuxième tournée aux États-Unis avec Karno.

1913 5 septembre : signe un contrat avec la Keystone Film Company. 29 novembre : dernière apparition sur scène avec la troupe de Karno.

1914 2 février : sortie de son premier film, *Pour gagner sa vie*. 7 février : sortie de *Charlot est content de lui*, le premier film où il endosse son célèbre costume. Février–décembre : apparaît dans 35 films pour Keystone. 14 décembre : sortie du *Roman comique de Charlot et Lolotte*, le premier long métrage burlesque.

1915 Réalise et interprète 14 films de deux bobines pour l'Essanay Film Manufacturing Company.

1916–1917 Produit, réalise et interprète 12 films de deux bobines distribués par la Mutual Film Corporation.

1918 Janvier : ouvre son propre studio. 23 octobre : épouse Mildred Harris.

1918–1922 Produit, réalise et interprète 8 films distribués par le First National Exhibitors' Circuit.

1919 5 février : création officielle de United Artists.

1920 30 novembre : Mildred Harris obtient le divorce.

1921 6 février : sortie du *Kid*, le premier long métrage de Chaplin. 3 septembre–12 octobre : retour triomphal en Europe.

1923 28 janvier : Chaplin et Pola Negri annoncent leurs fiançailles. 1er mars : rupture des fiançailles. 2 mars : le couple se fiance à nouveau. 28 juin : rupture définitive. 6 septembre : sortie du premier film de Chaplin pour United Artists, *L'Opinion publique*.

1924 26 novembre : épouse Lita Grey, dont il aura deux enfants, Charles Spencer (1925-1968) et Sydney Earl (né en 1926).

1927 12 août : Lita Grey obtient le divorce

1931 Premier film sonore de Chaplin, *Les Lumières de la ville*.

1931–1932 Grande tournée mondiale.

1932 Juillet : entame une liaison avec Paulette Goddard.

1936 17 février-3 juin : suite à la sortie des *Temps modernes*, il entreprend une grande tournée mondiale avec Paulette Goddard.

1940 15 octobre : sortie du premier film parlant de Chaplin, *Le Dictateur*.

1942 4 juin : Paulette Goddard obtient le divorce (le couple se serait marié en Extrême-Orient en 1936).

1943 16 juin : Chaplin épouse Oona O'Neill.

1944 10 février-14 avril : Chaplin a des démêlés avec la justice suite à sa liaison avec l'actrice Joan Barry. 13 décembre-2 janvier : procès en reconnaissance de paternité intenté par Joan Barry ; le jury ne parvient pas à trancher.

1945 4-17 avril : second procès en reconnaissance de paternité ; cette fois, le jury condamne Chaplin.

1952 17 septembre : Chaplin et sa famille embarquent pour Londres pour la première des *Feux de la rampe*. 19 septembre : son visa de retour aux États-Unis est annulé.

1953 Les Chaplin s'installent définitivement au Manoir de Ban à Corsier-sur-Vevey, en Suisse.

1957 12 septembre : première londonienne du premier film tourné par Chaplin en dehors de Hollywood, *Un roi à New York*.

1964 Publication de son autobiographie.

1967 Janvier : sortie de son dernier film, *La Comtesse de Hong-Kong*. Chaplin continuera à travailler jusqu'à sa mort, composant de nouvelles musiques pour ses films muets et préparant un scénario qui ne verra jamais le jour, *The Freak*.

1972 16 avril : il reçoit un oscar d'honneur à Hollywood.

1975 4 mars : il est fait chevalier par la reine Élisabeth II.

1977 25 décembre : Chaplin meurt dans son sommeil à son domicile.

1978 1er mars : le corps de Chaplin est dérobé dans

FAMILY CHRISTMAS CARD
Posing for a Christmas card. / Die Weihnachtskarte der Familie Chaplin. / La carte de vœux de la famille Chaplin.

sa tombe. Il est retrouvé le 17 mars ; Gantcho Ganev et Roman Wardas sont reconnus coupables.

1991 27 septembre : décès d'Oona Chaplin.

THE PAPER OF THE ENTERTAINMENT INDUSTRY

cinemaTV today

Why business is better by The Editor

(see page 5)

No. 9966. Saturday 5 February 1972   20p

chaplin's back!

CHARLIE CHAPLIN in MODERN TIMES U

WRITTEN, DIRECTED AND PRODUCED BY CHARLIE CHAPLIN

Distributed by BLACK INK FILMS LTD.

From Wednesday FEBRUARY 9 **PARAMOUNT**

LOWER REGENT STREET
839.6494

ROYAL CHARITY PREMIERE
in the presence of
H.R.H. PRINCESS ALEXANDRA
Tuesday February 8th at 7.30 for 8.15
to aid the Feathers Clubs Associati

4

FILMOGRAPHY

FILMOGRAFIE

FILMOGRAPHIE

All films star Charles Chaplin in the leading role, except for *A Woman of Paris* and *A Countess from Hong Kong*, in which he plays bit parts./In nahezu allen Filmen spielt Charles Chaplin die Hauptrolle. Ausnahmen sind: *Die Nächte einer schönen Frau* und *Die Gräfin von Hongkong*, in denen er nur kleine Nebenrollen übernimmt./Charlie Chaplin interprète le rôle principal dans l'ensemble des films, à l'exception de *L'Opinion publique* et de *La Comtesse de Hong-Kong*, où il tient un rôle de figurant.

The Keystone Films

Production/Produktionsgesellschaft/société de production: The Keystone Film Company. Producer/Produzent/producteur: Mack Sennett. Photography/Kamera/photographie: Keystone unit cameramen, including Frank D. Williams, E.J. Vallejo, Hans Koenekamp/Kamerateam von Keystone, darunter Frank D. Williams, E. J. Vallejo, Hans Koenekamp/cameramen de Keystone, notamment Frank D. Williams, E. J. Vallejo et Hans Koenekamp.

Making A Living/Man schlägt sich durch/Pour gagner sa vie (1914)

Kid Auto Races at Venice/Kid Auto Races at Venice/Charlot est content de lui (1914)

Mabel's Strange Predicament/Mabel's Strange Predicament/L'Étrange Aventure de Mabel (1914)

Between Showers/Between Showers/Charlot et le parapluie (1914)

A Film Johnnie/A Film Johnnie/Charlot fait du cinéma (1914)

Tango Tangles/Tango Tangles/Charlot danseur (1914)

His Favorite Pastime/His Favorite Pastime/Charlot entre le bar et l'amour (1914)

Cruel, Cruel Love/Cruel, Cruel Love/Charlot marquis (1914)

The Star Boarder/The Star Boarder/Charlot aime la patronne (1914)

Mabel at the Wheel/Mabel at the Wheel/Mabel au volant (1914)

Twenty Minutes of Love/Twenty Minutes of Love/ Charlot et le chronomètre (1914) Director & script/Regie u. Drehbuch/scénario et réalisation: Charles Chaplin.

Caught in a Cabaret/Caught in a Cabaret/ Charlot garçon de café (1914)

Caught in the Rain/Caught in the Rain/Charlot est encombrant (1914) Director & script/Regie u. Drehbuch/ scénario et réalisation: Charles Chaplin.

A Busy Day/A Busy Day/Madame Charlot (1914) Director & script/Regie u. Drehbuch/scénario et réalisation: Charles Chaplin.

The Fatal Mallet/The Fatal Mallet/Le Maillet de Charlot (1914)

The Knockout/The Knockout/Charlot et Fatty sur le ring (1914)

Mabel's Busy Day/Mabel's Busy Day/Charlot et les saucisses (1914)

Mabel's Married Life/Mabel's Married Life/Charlot et le mannequin (1914) Director/Regie/réalisation: Charles Chaplin. Script/Drehbuch/scénario:

Charles Chaplin, Mabel Normand. With/mit/avec: Mabel Normand, Mack Swain, Alice Howell.

Laughing Gas/Laughing Gas/Charlot dentiste (1914) Director & script/Regie u. Drehbuch/ scénario et réalisation: Charles Chaplin.

The Property Man/The Property Man/Charlot (1914) *garçon de théâtre* Director & script/Regie u. Drehbuch/scénario et réalisation: Charles Chaplin.

The Face on the Bar Room Floor/The Face on the Bar Room Floor/Charlot peintre (1914) Director/Regie /réalisation: Charles Chaplin.

Recreation/Recreation/Fièvre printanière (1914) Director & script/Regie u. Drehbuch/scénario et réalisation: Charles Chaplin.

The Masquerader/The Masquerader/Charlot grande coquette (1914) Director & script/Regie u. Drehbuch/scénario et réalisation: Charles Chaplin.

His New Profession/His New Profession/Charlot garde-malade (1914) Director & script/Regie u. Drehbuch/ scénario et réalisation: Charles Chaplin.

The Rounders/The Rounders/Charlot et Fatty font la bombe (1914) Director & script/Regie u. Drehbuch/ scénario et réalisation: Charles Chaplin.

The New Janitor/The New Janitor/Charlot concierge (1914) Director & script/Regie u. Drehbuch/ scénario et réalisation: Charles Chaplin.

Those Love Pangs/Those Love Pangs/Charlot rival d'amour (1914) Director & script/Regie u. Drehbuch/ scénario et réalisation: Charles Chaplin.

Dough and Dynamite/Dough and Dynamite/ Charlot mitron (1914) Director & script/Regie u. Drehbuch/scénario et réalisation: Charles Chaplin.

Gentlemen of Nerve/Gentlemen of Nerve/Charlot et Mabel aux courses (1914) Director & script/Regie u. Drehbuch/scénario et réalisation: Charles Chaplin.

His Musical Career/His Musical Career/Charlot déménageur (1914) Director & script/Regie u. Drehbuch/ scénario et réalisation: Charles Chaplin.

His Trysting Place/His Trysting Place/Charlot papa (1914) Director & script/Regie u. Drehbuch/ scénario et réalisation: Charles Chaplin.

Tillie's Punctured Romance/Tillie's Punctured Romance/Le Roman comique de Charlot et Lolotte (1914)

Getting Acquainted/Getting Acquainted/Charlot et Mabel en promenade (1914) Director & script/ Regie u. Drehbuch/scénario et réalisation: Charles Chaplin.

His Prehistoric Past/His Prehistoric Past/Charlot roi (1914) Director & script/Regie u. Drehbuch/ scénario et réalisation: Charles Chaplin.

The Essanay Films

Production/Produktionsgesellschaft/société de production: The Essanay Film Manufacturing Company. Producer/Produzent/producteur: Jesse T. Robbins. Director & script/Regie u. Drehbuch/ scénario et réalisation: Charles Chaplin. Photography/Kamera/photographie: Harry Ensign from *A Night Out* onwards/Harry Ensign ab *Eine verbummelte Nacht*/Harry Ensign à partir de *Charlot fait la noce* (photographer of *His New Job* unknown/*Charlie gegen alle*: unbekannt/ photographe pour *Charlot débute* : inconnu). Assistant Director/Regieassistenz/assistant-réalisateur: Ernest Van Pelt (from *His New Job*/ab *Charlie gegen alle*/à partir de *Charlot débute*). Scenic Artist/Bühnenbild/décors: E.T. Mazy (from *Work*/ab *Arbeit*/à partir de *Charlot apprenti*). Some authorities also credit George (Scotty) Cleethorpe as art director./Einige Quellen nennen auch George (Scotty) Cleethorpe als Bühnenbildner./Certaines sources citent également George (Scotty) Cleethorpe à la direction artistique.

His New Job/Charlie gegen alle/Charlot débute (1915)

A Night Out/Eine verbummelte Nacht/Charlot fait la noce (1915)

The Champion/The Champion/Charlot boxeur (1915)

In the Park/Im Park/Charlot dans le parc (1915)

A Jitney Elopement/Entführung/Charlot veut se marier (1915)

The Tramp/Der Tramp/Le Vagabond (1915)

By the Sea/An der See/Charlot à la plage (1915)

Work/Arbeit/Charlot apprenti (1915)

A Woman/Eine Frau/Mam'zelle Charlot (1915)

The Bank/Die Bank/Charlot à la banque (1915)

Shanghaied/Gekidnappt/Charlot marin (1915)

A Night in the Show/Eine Nacht im Varieté/Charlot au music-hall (1915)

Charlie Chaplin's Burlesque on Carmen/Charlie Chaplins Carmen-Parodie/Charlot joue Carmen (1916)

Police/Polizei/Charlot cambrioleur (1916)

The Mutual Films
Production/Produktionsgesellschaft/société de production: Lone Star Mutual. Producer, director & script/Produktion, Regie u. Drehbuch/scénario, réalisation et production: Charles Chaplin. Photography for *The Floorwalker, Fireman* and *Fireman/Kamera für Der Ladenaufseher, Der Feuerwehrmann* u. *Der Vagabund/* photographie pour *Charlot chef de rayon, Charlot pompier* et *Charlot musicien*: Frank D. Williams; assistant/Kameraassistenz/assistant: Roland Totheroh. Photography from *One A.M./Kamera ab Ein Uhr nachts*/photographie à partir de *Charlot rentre tard*: Roland Totheroh. Art Director/ Bühnenbild/direction artistique: George (Scotty) Cleethorpe.
Cast/Darsteller/distribution: Charles Chaplin, Edna Purviance, Eric Campbell, Albert Austin, John Rand, James T. Kelly, Henry Bergman (from *The Pawnshop*/ab *Das Pfandhaus*/à partir de *Charlot brocanteur*)

The Floorwalker/Der Ladenaufseher/Charlot chef de rayon (1916)

The Fireman/Der Feuerwehrmann/Charlot pompier (1916)

The Vagabond/Der Vagabund/Charlot musicien (1916)

One A.M./Ein Uhr nachts/Charlot rentre tard (1916)
Solo performance by Chaplin, with brief appearance by Albert Austin/Soloauftritt von Chaplin, mit einem Kurzauftritt von Albert Austin/interprétation en solo de Chaplin, avec une brève apparition d'Albert Austin.

The Count/Der Graf/Charlot et le comte (1916)

The Pawnshop/Das Pfandhaus/Charlot brocanteur (1916)

Behind the Screen/Hinter der Leinwand/ Le Machiniste (1916)

The Rink/Die Rollschuhbahn/Charlot patine (1916)

Easy Street/Leichte Straße/Charlot policeman (1917)

The Cure/Die Kur/Charlot fait une cure (1917)

The Immigrant/Der Einwanderer/L'Émigrant (1917)

The Adventurer/Der Abenteurer/Charlot s'évade (1917)

The First National Films
Production/Produktionsgesellschaft/société de production: Chaplin/First National. Producer, director & script/Produktion, Regie u. Drehbuch/ scénario, réalisation et production: Charles Chaplin. Photographer/Kamera/ photographie: Roland Totheroh; second camera/zweite Kamera/seconde caméra: Jack Wilson; assistant/ Kameraassistenz/assistant: Charles ('Chuck') Riesner. Production Designer/ Produktions-entwürfe/décors: Charles D. Hall. Filmed at the Chaplin Studio on Sunset and La Brea/Gedreht im Chaplin Studio am Sunset Boulevard, Ecke La Brea Avenue/tournés au Chaplin Studio, au coin de Sunset Bvd. et La Brea Ave.
Cast/Darsteller/distribution: Edna Purviance, Henry Bergman, Albert Austin, Tom Wilson.

How to Make Movies/Wie man Filme macht/How to Make Movies (1918)

A Dog's Life/Ein Hundeleben/Une vie de chien (1918)

The Bond/Die Anleihe/The Bond (1918)

Chaplin-Lauder Charity Film/Chaplin-Lauder-Wohltätigkeitsfilm/Film caritatif de Chaplin et Lauder (1918)

Shoulder Arms/Gewehr über!/Charlot soldat (1918)

Sunnyside/Auf der Sonnenseite/Une idylle aux champs (1919)

A Day's Pleasure/Vergnügte Stunden/Une journée de plaisir (1919)

The Kid/Der Vagabund und das Kind/Le Kid (1921)

The Idle Class/Die müßige Klasse/Charlot et le masque de fer (1921)

Pay Day/Zahltag/Jour de paie (1922)

The Pilgrim/Der Pilger/Le Pèlerin (1922)

The Professor/The Professor/The Professor (not completed/nicht fertig gestellt/inachevé. (1922)

The United Artists' Films
Distribution/Verleih/distribution: United Artists.
Producer, director & script/Produktion, Regie u.
Drehbuch/scénario, réalisation et production:
Charles Chaplin.

A Woman of Paris/Die Nächte einer schönen Frau/L'Opinion publique (1923)

The Gold Rush/Goldrausch/La Ruée vers l'or (1925)

The Circus/Der Zirkus/Le Cirque (1928)

City Lights/Lichter der Großstadt/Les Lumières de la ville (1931)

Modern Times/Moderne Zeiten/Les Temps modernes (1936)

The Great Dictator/Der große Diktator/Le Dictateur (1940)

Monsieur Verdoux/Monsieur Verdoux: Der Frauenmörder von Paris/Monsieur Verdoux (1947)

Limelight/Rampenlicht/Les Feux de la rampe (1952)

The British Productions
Producer, director, script & music/Produktion,
Regie, Drehbuch u. Musik/scénario, réalisation,
production et musique: Charles Chaplin

A King in New York/Ein König in New York/Un roi à New York (1957)

A Countess from Hong Kong/Die Gräfin von Hongkong/La Comtesse de Hong-Kong (1967)

BIBLIOGRAPHY

Asplund, Uno: *Chaplin's Films.* Translated by Paul Britten Austin, David & Charles, 1973.
Bazin, André: *Charlie Chaplin.* Preface by François Truffaut, Editions du Cerf, 1973.
Bessy, Maurice: *Charlie Chaplin.* Harper Collins, 1985.
Chaplin, Charles: *My Autobiography.* Simon and Schuster, 1964.
Chaplin, Charles: *My Life in Pictures.* Introduction by Francis Wyndham, Grosset & Dunlap, 1976.
Chaplin, Charles, Jr. (with N. and M. Rau): *My Father, Charlie Chaplin.* Random House, 1960.
Chaplin, Lita Grey (with Jeffrey Vance): *Wife of the Life of the Party.* Foreword by Sydney Chaplin, Scarecrow Press, 1998.
Chaplin, Michael: *I Couldn't Smoke the Grass on My Father's Lawn.* Putnam's Sons, 1966.
Comte, Michel: *Charlie Chaplin: A Photo Diary.* Steidl, 2002.
Cotes, Peter and Niklaus, Thelma: *The Little Fellow: The Life and Work of Charles Spencer Chaplin.* Foreword by W. Somerset Maugham, Philosophical Library Inc., 1951.
Epstein, Jerry: *Remembering Charlie.* Bloomsbury, 1988.
Eriksson, Lennart: *Books on/by Chaplin.* Lennart Eriksson, 1980.
Gehring, Wes D.: *Charlie Chaplin: A Bio-Bibliography.* Greenwood Press, 1983.
Gifford, Denis: *Chaplin.* Macmillan, 1974.
Haining, Peter: *The Legend of Charlie Chaplin.* W. H. Allen, 1983.
Hale, Georgia (Heather Kiernan Ed.): *Charlie Chaplin: Intimate Close-Ups.* Scarecrow Press, 1995.
Huff, Theodore: *Charlie Chaplin.* Henry Schuman, 1952.
Kimber, John: *The Art of Charlie Chaplin.* Sheffield Academic Press, 2000.
Lynn, Kenneth S.: *Charlie Chaplin and his Times.* Simon and Schuster, 1997.
Lyons, Timothy J.: *Charles Chaplin: A Guide to References and Resources.* G.K. Hall, 1979.
McCabe, John: *Charlie Chaplin.* Doubleday, 1974.

McCaffrey, Donald W.: *Focus on Chaplin.* Prentice-Hall, 1971.
McDonald, Gerald D., Conway, Michael and Ricci, Mark: *The Films of Charlie Chaplin.* Citadel Press, 1965.
Maland, Charles J.: *Chaplin and American Culture.* Princeton University Press, 1989.
Manvell, Roger: *Chaplin.* Introduction by J. H. Plumb, Hutchinson, 1974.
Martin, Marcel: *Charles Chaplin.* Editions Seghers, 1966.
Mehran, Hooman and Scheide, Frank (Eds.): *The Chaplin Review: I. The Dictator and the Tramp.* British Film Institute, 2004.
Mehran, Hooman and Scheide, Frank (Eds.): *The Chaplin Review. II. Chaplin's Limelight and the Music Hall Tradition.* McFarland, 2006.
Minney, R.J.: *Chaplin: The Immortal Tramp.* George Newnes, 1954.
Mitchell, Glenn: *The Chaplin Encyclopaedia.* Batsford, 1997.
Mitry, Jean: *Tout Chaplin.* Editions Seghers, 1972.
Payne, Robert: *The Great Charlie.* Foreword by G.W. Stonier, Hermitage House, 1952.
Quigley, Isabel: *Charlie Chaplin, Early Comedies.* Studio Vista, 1968.
Robinson, David: *Chaplin: The Mirror of Opinion.* Secker and Warburg, 1983.
Robinson, David: *Chaplin: His Life and Art.* McGraw-Hill, 1985.
Robinson, David: *Charlie Chaplin: The Art of Comedy.* Thames and Hudson, 1996.
Ross, Lillian: *Moments with Chaplin.* Dodd, Mead and Company, 1978.
Sadoul, Georges: *Vie de Charlot. Charles Spencer Chaplin, ses films et son temps.* Les Editeurs Français Réunis, 1952.
Sobel, Raoul and Francis, David: *Chaplin, Genesis of a Clown.* Horizon Press, 1974.
Tyler, Parker: *Chaplin, Last of the Clowns.* Vanguard Press, 1947.
von Ulm, Gerith: *Charlie Chaplin, King of Tragedy: An Unauthorized Biography.* Caxton Printers, 1940.

IMPRINT

© 2006 TASCHEN GmbH
Hohenzollernring 53, D-50672 Köln
www.taschen.com

Editor/Picture Research/Layout: Paul Duncan/Wordsmith Solutions
Editorial Coordination: Martin Holz, Cologne
Production Coordination: Nadia Najm and Horst Neuzner, Cologne
German translation: Thomas J. Kinne, Nauheim
French translation: Anne Le Bot, Paris
Multilingual production: www.arnaudbriand.com, Paris
Typeface Design: Sense/Net, Andy Disl and Birgit Reber, Cologne

Printed in Italy

ISBN-13: 978-3-8228-2005-6
ISBN-10: 3-8228-2005-9

To stay informed about upcoming TASCHEN titles, please request our magazine at www.taschen.com/magazine or write to TASCHEN, Hohenzollernring 53, D-50672 Cologne, Germany, contact@taschen.com, Fax: +49-221-254919. We will be happy to send you a free copy of our magazine which is filled with information about all of our books.

Copyright
All the images in this book except for those listed below, were supplied by the Association Chaplin and are the property of Roy Export Company Establishment. All images from Chaplin films made from 1918 onwards, Copyright © Roy Export Company Establishment. Charles Chaplin and the Little Tramp are trademarks and/or service marks of Bubbles Inc. S.A. and/or Roy Export Company Establishment, used with permission.

The Kobal Collection, London/New York: pp. 16, 17, 21, 32, 36, 44, 51, 53, 56, 59, 61, 69, 94, 190, 191
The David Robinson Collection: pp. 40, 81, 95, 188
The Jim Heimann Collection: pp. 136/137
W. Eugene Smith/Black Star: p. 167
Yves Debraine: p. 185

HMNTW 791
.4302
8
C464R

ROBINSON, DAVID,
   CHAPLIN

MONTROSE
08/07